Never Say, "Can't":

Memoir of a Successful Woman

Never Say, "Can't":

Memoir of a Successful Woman

Wanda Novak

iUniverse, Inc.
Bloomington

Never Say, "Can't": Memoir of a Successful Woman

iUniverse books may be ordered through booksellers or by contacting:

iUniverse
1663 Liberty Drive
Bloomington, IN 47403
www.iuniverse.com
1-800-Authors (1-800-288-4677)

ISBN: 978-1-4759-4351-1 (sc)
ISBN: 978-1-4759-4352-8 (ebk)

Printed in the United States of America

iUniverse rev. date: 08/27/2012

Archimedes, one of the leading scientists in classical antiquity is purported to have stated, "Give me a place to stand, and I will move the world." I am telling you that, for me, there is truth in that statement. Establishing a position, holding it, being productive from that position, it is a wonderful feeling. By holding a position, a being can achieve much, as a mom, an employee, an employer, whatever. Being knocked off that position by outside influences or one's own bumbling ineptness, unable to get right back up, that's not so much fun. However, live, learn, and get back up we must.

I am reminded of one hot, dry, dusty, midmorning of another summer day in Nebraska. I didn't mind the heat or the dust. I was enjoying myself. With car windows rolled down, the breeze was enough to cool the body. As for the dust, you just learn to live with it. My attention was extroverted, on the road, on the hills. A bit in the distance sat a charming, country schoolhouse. It held my attention momentarily.

Suddenly, I am being tossed about. Right side up, upside down. I am bouncing around inside the car, then half in, half out of it. There was no time to think, "What's happening?" There was no thought of, "Damn, this is going to mess up my day." None of that.

In seconds I went from pleasure, to confusion, to excruciating pain. If not for the Grace of God and . . .

Wanda Novak, 2008—
Machu Picchu Ruins, Peru

The mountain at my back is Pachamama.
Local lore says this is the heart of the planet.
If one looks closely, the mountain is shaped like a heart,
and the fault lines seem to be veins.

Introduction

Wanda Novak, who is she?

Ms. Novak hails from a small, High Plains farming community. She was raised on an Indian reservation in Nebraska. Her mother, a renaissance woman, was a recognized registered nurse and anesthetist. During her career, her mother cared for people on Indian reservations all over the Central Plains. She also practiced public health nursing at major hospitals in Houston and Chicago.

Though possessing only a fifth-grade education, Wanda's father was a successful cow trader, rancher, and farmer. Her mother and father married late in life. From the age of three or four, her parents instilled a tough work ethic and they were never soft on their only child. Wanda was never allowed to say the word "can't," but was instilled with independence and self-reliance.

Wanda, then Miss French, earned her first significant income raising 4-H calves (age ten). She was a champion figure skater making her way to Nationals at age fourteen, fifteen, and sixteen. Upon graduation from high school, at sixteen, her parents gave her $50 and told her to never come back for any more money. Wanda worked at the university while attending Kansas State. She has since continued her education in numerous fields including banking, advertising, broadcast, public relations, real estate, property appraisal, farming, ranching, veterinary work, business consulting, training and coaching; investments, commodities and stock brokering.

Wanda was the first woman livestock market-reporter on a major livestock terminal in Omaha. She also worked at Skelly Oil as an assistant to the vice president of advertising, working with network radio and TV shows that Skelly Oil sponsored. Later, Wanda was executive assistant to the richest man in Kansas. She worked with him in over twenty corporations that he owned throughout the United States.

Wanda worked in advertising, broadcast, and public relations in Austin, TX. She was helping with President Kennedy's trip to Austin when he was killed in Dallas. She continued her work in advertising, broadcast, and public relations with projects for President Lyndon Johnson and Governor John Connally. During that time, Wanda originated the first written tour of the Texas Capitol in Austin; it is believed this text is being used to this day.

Wanda worked with several movie stars handling Public Relations for John Wayne's *Alamo, Who Shot Liberty Valance,* the public appearances of TV stars from *Bonanza* and *Gunsmoke,* as well as many well-known night club entertainers.

Returning to the Omaha area, she worked in advertising and public relations. Wanda was the first woman vice president of a major ad agency in Omaha and, later, the first woman to sell television advertising time in the United States. At a time when the industry and the media were totally male-dominated, Ms. Novak, now widely known as "Wonderful Wanda," was the Top Producer in her field.

For seven years Wanda worked in advertising by day then she tended a herd of four-hundred mother cows, a feedlot of one-hundred twenty head, and played the commodities market for another ten to twelve hours of the day, seven days a week. This is how she took her annual income from $4,200 to over $500,000 in just seven years.

After a series of personal tragedies she began a study of life and the spirit. In this pursuit she traveled to various countries examining the subjects of life and death. She delved into several spiritual studies in the United States. Today, she continues her pursuits of knowledge and matters of the spirit as well as business.

Bringing her unique work ethic and perspectives into focus during the mid-1990s, Wanda Novak created a coaching and training company (before it became such a popular profession) where she met and worked with several well-know personalities and celebrities from the High Plains to the cities of Dallas-Fort Worth, and parts in between.

Wanda is presently in Florida designing her next book and planning a lecture tour around this one. Wanda's activities are now about, as she says, "Giving back." Among the things she would like to talk about are the "9 Incredible Tools Smart People Use to Get What They Want." The nine "tools" are introduced herein.

I hope this introduction gives sufficient reason to read the book, and we hope the book gives compelling reason to lend an ear when Wonderful Wanda comes to your area.

Ted Crammer
Editor

Prologue

One day when I was still young, I realized that no female on either side of my family had lived past the age of fifty. I assumed that would be my fate as well. I decided to set my life goals star high. Then wasting no time, I passionately reached for them. However, in the back of my mind, I held fifty as my cutoff point.

Here I am today, fifty and then some. What a surprise! Either the gods are playing a huge joke on me, or there is another reason why I am still here. I choose to think there's another reason, a good reason. Every morning as I awake and feel my feet hit the floor, I thank God for the gift of life. I finally realized that my mission here in this life won't be complete until I have shared some of the things I have learned along my way. I hope to be around for quite a while because I have a great deal to share.

I should begin by defining *success*. If finding and marrying the love of your life is your idea of success, then I have been successful. If having your own flourishing business is your idea of success, then I have been successful. If flying your own airplane is your idea of success, then I have been successful. If driving an expensive car such as my Maserati is your idea of success, then I have been successful. If consistently leading all other salespeople on your company's stat board is your idea of success, then I have been successful. If earning a million dollars is your idea of success, then I have been successful. If world travel . . . Well, you get the idea.

To me, *success* means reaching for and achieving my goals. Some people have attained status, wealth, or other things that many of us would label as success, yet some of those same people find no joy in what they have attained. I have known a few people like that. They became a doctor, lawyer, engineer, or something else, primarily to please another, not to please themselves. Some people reach a goal, but it's not their own goal. This, too, can lead to no joy. I would have to add that *success* means setting and reaching *one's own goals* and, though the challenges may be difficult and many, one remains energized by his or her goals and expectations.

My life hasn't been one, long successful rise to the stars. Like many other people I know, I've had my ups and downs. My highs have been very high by almost any standard, higher than many people will ever achieve. In contrast, my lows have been very low, lower than many people will ever have to experience. Between the extremes of high and low, life always handed me a lesson. It was my responsibility to figure out what that lesson was, then deal with it.

Dictionary Use

For clarity sake, I have taken to defining a few key words throughout the text. I used several different dictionaries, then I focused on exact definitions within those volumes that expressed what I wanted to say. Modern dictionaries aren't always the best, in my estimation. Though it is nearly one-hundred years since its last printing, I enjoy *The Century Dictionary*. It's big; it's beautiful; it's comprehensive. Also, it is available for free, on-line. Referring to it facilitates a wonderful, liberal education that won't cost a person anything but time and attention.

A person could begin, as I have done, by looking up any word that grabs his or her curiosity. If there is a word in the definition that they don't fully comprehend, they would look that up, too.

Over the years, some of the words I chose to delve into were: power, will, individual, spirit, intention, purpose, prosperity, life, liberty, happiness, responsibility, and more.

Coaching

I refer to coaches and coaching throughout the book. Most of us know about coaches in sports activities; I had a skating coach when I was young. There are many styles of coaching, and any subject or activity can be coached. A good coach is able to impart experience, craft, guidance, inspiration, and so on. The best coaches, in my estimation, are also able to bring forth (educe) the best qualities and performance resident within the student.

My father coached me in the care and handling of calves as well as other farm animals. He coached me on buying and selling livestock—and other subjects. My mother coached me in public speaking, manners, self-defense, and more. This style of coaching is probably the most common type. It is often presented as a small bit of eduction occasioned by a great deal of indoctrination. For the most part, my early coaches told me about the subjects they wanted me to understand, enough to elicit my participation. They didn't ask for my thoughts on the matter, just my performance.

Compare *educe* with *indoctrinate*.

There is another form of coaching that depends primarily on eduction with a minimal amount of indoctrination. This style allows an individual to examine his or her own thoughts and experience, draw their own conclusions, then set their own course for the future. This method is aimed at bringing out what is best in a person. Most often when I refer to "speaking with my coach," this is the style of consultation I am referring to.

The earliest known form of fostering critical thinking is called the Socratic method. The focus is on giving students good, probing questions, not answers. With continued probing into a subject, an inquiring mind can come to evaluate, accepting or rejecting on one's own determinism, what is important to the person, and what is not.

This style of coaching is direct and businesslike, yet warm and friendly. It is compassionate, but unforgiving in quest for truth. A good coach is skilled at holding one's feet to the fire until a particular matter (difficulty, upset, goal, etc.) has been resolved. You are very lucky if you can find such a coach as this particular person will allow you to have your own thoughts and feelings without stepping all over them while you sort things out. The following quote works very well in describing the coach and student relationship:

But oh! the blessing it is to have a friend to whom one can speak fearlessly on any subject; with whom one's deepest as well as one's most foolish thoughts come out simply and safely. Oh, the comfort—the inexpressible comfort of feeling safe with a person—having neither to weigh thoughts nor measure words, but pouring them all right out, just as they are, chaff and grain together; certain that a faithful hand will take and sift them, keep what is worth keeping, and then with the breath of kindness blow the rest away. — Dinah Craik, A Life for a Life, (1859)

Acknowledgments

Thank you to my many teachers:

- Mildred French, for always being there when I most needed help;
- Ervin French, for unwavering stability and support in our family life;
- Samuel "Grandpa" French, for giving me his pioneer spirit; for teaching me lessons of life and death on the High Plains;
- Jay Durnil, for showing me how incredibly capable children really are;
- Jerry Durnil, for placing me in situations where I had no choice but to excel;
- Nathan Novak, the gentle man who taught me about unconditional love;
- Ruth Olinger, my grade school teacher. Besides required subjects, she taught bridge, chess, and drawing because outside interests were important to her;
- Irene Siefert, whose first lesson was, perhaps, the most important, "Roll when you fall." Thank you for bringing out the champion in me;
- August Palmasano, who taught me what it means to work with partners, particularly those who possess different styles;
- Sue Hollins, for coaching that helped me get though the biggest challenge of my life; for continued support throughout the years;
- Russ Daub, my friend, my lawyer, also one on a spiritual path;
- Terry Germer, my real estate appraisal coach and professional confidant;

- John Galusha, one of my spiritual coaches and trainers. John was an extraordinary gentleman; he laughed and cried with me, he helped me over the next big challenge of my life;
- Murray Chopping, a marvelous life coach who, over a 4 year period, helped me expand my perceptions and accelerate my knowledge of life and living;
- Rabbi Allan Kaiser, for helping me with the bad guys, also for teaching me about the many facets of religion expressed on this planet;
- Father Justin Belitz, for his insights on life and living, also for his instruction in Sylvia Mind Development;
- Eunice Navieux, precious friend, seeker of knowledge, she walks to the beat of a different drummer;
- Susan Worley, seeker of knowledge, a friend I can talk to about anything. She makes it "okay" and I'm never made to feel wrong, even if I am. She is a precious being;
- Lola Wollery, steadfast friend, teammate in spiritual adventures;
- Shirley Matthews, friend, life coach; she helped me over a major setback which opened the door to writing this book;
- Mike Myers, business partner, steadfast supporter of my crazy impulses;
- Ted Crammer, who, when I said, "I am thinking about writing a book," asked, "What is there to think about?" Ted coached and encouraged me while committing these thoughts to paper.

Dedicated to Mom and Dad
who insured my good start in life.

TABLE OF CONTENTS

Presence

As we let our light shine, we consciously give other people
permission to do the same. As we are liberated from our own
fear, our presence actually liberates others.
— Marianne Williamson[1]

A person of good will can work wonders
in human relationships when he or she
is able to look another in the eye with
calmness and certainty, then speak the
truth as he or she perceives it. In life,
maintaining a high level of presence will
open many doors that would otherwise
have remained closed. For one thing, in
being present a person is more likely to
notice opportunities when they present
themselves. When this photo was taken I
was in a studio supervising some models

at a photo shoot. The photographer called out my name, I turned
to him, then he quickly snapped this picture.

Unbeknownst to me, in a few weeks, I would be having cocktails
and chatting with Princess Margaret and Prince Charles. In the
following week, while touring the Vatican, I seized an opportunity

---

[1] *A Return to Love, Reflections on the Principles of A Course in
Miracles*

and managed to receive a blessing by the Pope. It was a matter of being in the right place at the right time, not being too bashful to include myself in the happenings of the moment. I still have the lovely, wooden rosary the Pope gave me. It hangs above the head of my bed.

The Century Dictionary defines *present* as follows: 1. Being or abiding, as a person, in this or any specified place; being in view or immediately at hand: opposed to *absent*, 2. Now existing; being at this time; not in the past or future, 3. Being now in mind, 4. Prompt or ready at need.

So what is *Presence*?

The Century Dictionary defines *presence* as follows: 1. The state of being present in a certain place, and not in some other place; being, continuance, or stay in a certain place . . .

In contrast, *The Century Dictionary* defines *absent* as follows: 1. Not in a certain place at a given time; not in consciousness or thought at a certain time; away; opposed to present, 2. Not existing; wanting; not forming a part or attribute of: as, among them refinement is *absent.*

Some people drag themselves to work, punch a time clock, look busy or just plain goof-off throughout the day, then punch out. This often passes as normal presence, even though accomplishing a minimum of work. Yet, that level of presence is so low, it qualifies as a liability to the employer who probably thinks he has a position filled with productive potential. Under such a circumstance, the employer probably doesn't have the position filled to anywhere near viable capacity. Furthermore, if absent employees are working around dangerous machinery, their condition makes them a liability to themselves as well.

On the other hand, some people are willing and able to collect themselves up in body, thought, and spirit, then present the complete package to the task at hand. That is Presence.

Here's an example of exercising presence from my own life: I was the first woman "salesman" selling TV ad time in the interior United States. I was confronted with all the usual prejudice of that time when business was considered a man's game, and women served best at home.

One day I received a memo from my boss concerning my sales for the past quarter; it was not favorable. He wasn't pleased with my performance, and demanded a 15 percent increase in sales volume. My boss was one of those people who felt women didn't belong in positions traditionally held by men.

Not to be dominated or outdone, but to maintain control over my own situation, I immediately decided to increase my sales by 35 percent. I went home, still determined to increase my sales well above expectations. As I reviewed my possibilities, I decided to increase my productivity by 50 percent. Why? The answer is simple: I am competitive, and I wanted to maintain control over my own situation while outdoing the men on the sales team.

The first novel made for a TV series was scheduled to come out on CBS, Testimony of Two Men, (1977, Taylor Caldwell). The series would run a total of fifteen hours show time, on prime-time TV. One of my accounts was with a large bank in the area. As fifteen hours represented a large advertising expenditure, above and beyond the bank's annual budget costs, I asked my sales manager to accompany me on the call.

The proposal I wrote was for thirty-four *additional* prime-time commercials. We gave our presentation. I put the contract in front of the president of the bank, then I asked for the order. The salespeople among you probably know the applicable maxim at this stage of the sale: Shut up, because he who speaks first loses.

In those days it was acceptable and common to smoke in the office. The president lit his cigarette, then smoked it slowly as if thinking out his decision. He smoked for twenty minutes. I remained comfortable, but I noticed my sales manager fidgeting; he opened his mouth to speak, so I kicked him hard under the table. At that strong signal, my manager remained quiet.

Finally, the bank president said, "Let's go to lunch while I think about it." I pushed the contract and pen closer to him. Then I said, "Sign the paperwork now and we'll have a better, more expensive lunch." Again I remained silent. The bank manager said, "I know what you're doing. I took the same Dale Carnegie Course." I smiled, said nothing, but maintained eye-to-eye contact. I pushed the contract and pen even closer.

The bank manager picked up the pen, signed the contract, looked at my sales manager then said, "John, this girl is damn good." I'm convinced we'll be here in silence 'til supper if I don't sign this." We all laughed.

The station rewarded our sales team with a trip to Las Vegas. On my right Al Hall, on my left John Dixon, Bob Metz, Howie Anderson with a friend who didn't work at the station, John Marques, Ed Trimble, and Ed Zachary. Johnny Carson was the headliner. He had once worked at our station and an old engineer friend tipped him on our arrival. Johnny gave us about fifteen minutes of attention and worked us over as comedians do. Since my nickname was "Wonderful Wanda" and I was there with eight guys, Johnny had a good time poking fun at that.

The closure of that sale hinged on nothing more than being comfortably present, doing nothing else, not even thinking anything else, while continuing eye contact with businesslike friendliness.

See how being present can help any sales person? There were one-hundred eighty commercial slots in that TV series. Even though there were local and national reps also on the job, I sold one-hundred twenty-four of those commercials, plus maintained my regular business. After all the numbers were tallied, I was awarded "salesman of the month."

These successes and many more begin by collecting oneself up in body, thought, and spirit, then presenting the entire package to the task at hand. *That is Presence.*

Many years ago I attended a talk given at my church by a man who introduced me to *confronting*. I don't remember his name. I don't know where he was from or if he represented some organization. Yet, I remember he sat us down face-to-face, then told us, "I want you to be here." He didn't give us anything to study; he just told us what to do. When he sat down in front of me to see how I was doing, he said that he felt very comfortable in my presence.

My parents taught me to always look another in the eye when speaking with them, so confronting has always been comfortable for me. Nevertheless, after that training session, I noticed that most people don't look another in the eye when they are talking. That workshop started me looking for different things I could study about confronting as a subject.

To confront means to face up to, to stand face to face with, preferably in comfort. If comfort is not available, one confronts anyway. To address life situations, to move forward in life, confronting is both necessary and practical. People who won't confront end up having many problems.

Though a situation may be stressful, though a communication may be difficult to receive or deliver, a being must set aside all fears, then deal with what's at hand. Having confronted that which should be confronted, a person usually feels lighter, uplifted. In the business of building a life, to confront is ultimately easier and more rewarding than to not confront.

In comparison, I would say *presence* is a refinement on confronting as *presence* involves being with, not just facing. It is noteworthy that one person being present with another tends to pull the other into a state of greater presence. This is a situation where the power of two becomes much greater than the sum of each alone. If you can recall a time when you were in really good communication with someone, when you really liked that someone, when you knew you were understood and understanding of each other, you have recalled a moment of presence. In rare moments, this presence is so profound that time seems to stand still; the sun might go down and the sun might rise, but for the people involved it seems as though mere seconds have passed.

As I applied myself to the business of living and attaining my goals, I started to prosper. I took an inventory: There was my house surrounded by acres of land, investments in corn, cattle, silver, and gold. Now was the time to diversify into diamonds. Diamonds are highly portable. I read that some of the Jewish people in Germany during WWII possessed diamonds that they were able to use as payment for passage out of the country. I perceived the value of precious stones beyond glitz and glitter, so I thought that might be a good investment for me, too.

My search led me to books about diamonds, then conversations with people who bought, held, sold, and traded them. I tried to study weight, color, brilliance, and how to recognize flaws. I spoke with several people who recommended a specific jeweler in Omaha; he was well-known as honest and knowledgeable. This would be a good contact. His name was Ike.

My first investment opportunity came at an estate sale where a 2.3 carat, Old Mine Cut diamond was offered.[2] It had a significant flaw. I paid $300 for the diamond. When I went into Ike's store, I told him that I wanted the flaw removed, and perhaps a rose cut for the stone. Ike told me that it would become a smaller stone; he would do his best. Our meeting was brief. Ike was present with me, listening and understanding exactly what I wanted. When the cut was finished, Ike handed me a 1.65 carat stone with an E

---

[2] The Old Mine Cut is the earliest form of the "brilliant cut" diamond.

Color Brilliance.[3] He explained that its value as a non-mounted stone would be around $1,500.

When I went back to Ike's store to get a mounting, Ike was nowhere in sight, but a clerk was in the front of the store. The clerk offered little help, only looking at the jewelry, never looking at me. We never connected so I did not have a good feeling about him or that he was making an effort to help anyone but himself. Most importantly, he was not showing me what I wanted. Of course, in his defense, I didn't know what I wanted, but he was never *with* me, to help me find out. "Oh," I thought, "I'll come back another time. I'm just looking." Then, verbalizing my thought, I started to walk out.

My hand was on the door when from behind me I heard, "I really have a deal for you today." It was Ike.

I explained to Ike that I wanted a mounting and, in his attentive style, he listened. Of the hundreds of mountings Ike had available, he chose to show me one that looked like a golden pine cone. My diamond would fit perfectly.

Then Ike showed me a "Stopper." It was a designer ring with twenty-one diamonds, each mounted on a different level. The base formed a flame of fire with a diamond on top. The ring was about an inch high on my finger; the base extended to my first knuckle. It was big. It was bold, like a headlight on an old Rolls-Royce. The twenty-one diamonds totaled 3.45 carats. I said, "If we take out the top seven stones, my stone will fit."

---

[3]   An "E" Color Grade diamond contains minute traces of Color maintaining an exceptionally high level of brilliance and is considered very rare. The "E" Color diamond is the second highest Color grade a diamond can achieve.

Ike's fingers were magic; he almost caressed the ring. He looked me in the eyes and said, "Wanda, no one will have a ring like this in all of Omaha, maybe not anywhere. It will knock many a woman's eyes out—there's so much flash. Let's take it outside in the sunlight."

Standing outside in the bright light, I could see that the ring did have significant fire.

We walked back into the store. Eye to eye, I asked Ike the price of the "Stopper" with the top seven stones removed. He told me. Armed with the knowledge of a jeweler's typical markup, I agreed to the price he quoted, but only if he left the seven top stones in place.

Then, I offered to pay half-price for the pine cone mounting that he had shown me earlier. Ike gave me his best Jewish Merchant communication. We both stood eye to eye for a few moments. I said nothing, just listened to his patter. He finally said, "Okay," and both of us had struck a fair deal.

That was the beginning of a long, prosperous relationship. Over the years, I bought many diamonds as well as gold and collector's coins from him. Twice when I was in need of ready cash, I pawned the stones with him. Ike always gave me the money I needed. He never charged me interest. So, I continued to be a loyal customer. I referred many of my friends to Ike. They were loyal customers for the same reasons I was.

That obnoxious ring eventually took new form as a square, obnoxious bracelet. The ring appraised at $12,000. It's not surprising. Ike told me I would make money on it. His store grew and grew as word-of-mouth spread. People came from all over the United States to do business with him. Ike would always come out from the back of the shop to give me a deal when I came in.

Our relationship only ended when Ike became ill, then sold out to Berkshire-Hathaway, a Warren Buffet holding company.

A twenty-five-year, prosperous relationship grew out of our first meeting because someone was present and helped me get what I wanted.

In spite of my many achievements, the image I hold of myself is that of being a farm girl from Nebraska. My parents and grandparents gave me my name, my fundamental work ethic, and much of my initial appreciation of life. Now I'd like to tell you a bit about meeting Princess Margaret:

In 1970, I was in England for a business convention, the First International Convention of American Women in Radio and Television. It was a huge event. One-thousand women from the United States, Canada, Europe, the Middle East, and one woman from India attended. All of them were strong women, all with some influence in broadcasting, advertising, or public relations.

The first night there we registered for the convention. Registration was followed by a mixer. Other people from England also attended the mixer, including the press. At the time, there were around thirty newspapers in London. I was somewhat attractive in those days; three reporters came over to talk to me.

When they found out that I owned and operated a ranch, flew my own airplane, and was the vice president of an advertising agency, they were all excited. I didn't see for myself, but I heard from some others that I was written up in three London papers. They printed a photograph of me, too.

Not everyone from the convention received an invitation. I have a hunch that one of Princess Margaret's aides saw one of the news articles. That's how I was selected. The reception was at Lancaster House, St. James. "Informal dress" was specified.

The Nebraska farm girl chose to wear a street length, white-lace evening suit with rhinestone buttons. My outfit was very proper, with a button-to-the-neck jacket, several diamond rings, cuff links, and a bracelet valued at, perhaps, $50,000.

All the guests stood in a U-shaped line waiting to greet Princess Margaret as she moved by. Before we met, the Princess seemed to recognize me in the line. When she finally stood in front of me, she said a few things that nearly bowled me over; her comments were quite unexpected. She knew my background. She recognized me as being a busy woman and " . . . doing all you do. We really need women like you in this country."

After our brief meeting, I felt she must be saying something similar to everyone she met that night. Then, I noticed that she shook everyone's hand and said, "Hello," but she spent additional time with only four people. I was one of them. As to her presence with me, she was totally there!

Prince Charles, on the other hand, appeared largely absent. He moved a step behind the Princess. All he did was nod and smile. It looked as though he would have rather been any place but there with all those women.

Notes:

Notes:

Purpose

Purpose is the reason for *presence*.

To forget one's purpose is the commonest form of stupidity.
– Friedrich Nietzsche[4]

The *American Heritage Dictionary* defines *Purpose* as follows: 1. The object toward which one strives or for which something exists; an aim or a goal, 2. A result or effect that is intended or desired; an intention. Determination; resolution: He was a man of *purpose*, 3. The matter at hand; the point at issue.

At one time I had four-hundred mother cows, plus several bulls in my herd. To solve the problem of where to keep them, I contracted with local farmers to range the herd on their fields during the winter months. In this situation the cows served as cleaners. By the cows feeding off of the fields, the farmers didn't have volunteer corn coming up the following spring.[5] This saved money on herbicides, with the added benefit of the cows leaving a natural fertilizer as they worked.

The herd grazed over 3,000 acres. The manual labor in this arrangement was primarily in putting up and taking down fence. When it came time to ready the fields for planting, the farmers often gave us little or no notice, leaving us in a rush to remove the herd and fencing.

---

[4]   Friedrich Nietzsche, 19th-century German philosopher

[5]   Volunteer corn is considered a weed.

As I recall it was a Thursday. My hired man and I discussed getting the cows out of a 640-acre farm during the coming weekend. We would need to corral the cattle, load and transport them in trailers to our headquarters. Being farmland, there were no corrals on the property, so we would have to bring our own. There was, however, a very large barn sitting on the top of a hill in the middle of the section. We formulated a plan, then made ready to move the herd.

That night I received a call from the farmer: The cows had to be moved out immediately as he planned to begin farming that property the next afternoon!

These are range cows roaming 640 acres! They are not tame! WOW! What a challenge!

This is the way I see it: For most of us, it is an easy chore to form a purpose in one's own mind. You simply conclude, "I want . . ." Or, "I would like to . . ." Or, "I will . . ." Or, you formulate some other proposition with an activity and goal in mind. So stated, the purpose can stand alone, unencumbered by counter-purposes or cross-purposes. Yet, living is often a process of navigating a multiplicity of purposes—one's own, as well as those coming from others.

In any case, success requires confront, communication, and management skill. This was my situation: My primary purpose as a rancher crossed with the farmer's purpose and expectations. I had to act!

First, I asked for help! I called three friends who had access to large stock-trailers. With these added to my two trailers, one large gooseneck and a small twelve-footer, I called my hired man to alert him of the long day ahead of us. We would meet at 6 a.m. to load the few corral panels that we had, then head on over to the farm.

Friday morning, we loaded the panels in the larger of the two trailers. I followed my hired man to the farm in my new Cadillac.

When we arrived, we headed out across the property to the barn on the hilltop. There, we unloaded our panels and dropped the big trailer. We formed a corral at the big-door entrance to the barn. Then, my hired man headed back to our headquarters to get the smaller trailer and some sweet-feed.

Our friends started arriving with their trailers between 8 and 9 a.m. We arranged the trailers, pickups, and my Cadillac as part of the corral.

Two of the guys went out on horseback to herd the individuals into small groups of cows. Then, they assembled the small groups into a single, large group. As we were working, the sky above opened up. We worked in the mud. Between brief rain showers and falling snow, we sheltered ourselves in the barn.

With our makeshift corral complete, we stood ready, but didn't wait long. The guys on horseback herded the cows at the bottom of the hill. I knew we had but one chance to get the herd into the makeshift enclosure. Our work would get difficult beyond measure should one cow or bull could get out. I let the guys know what I expected.

I stepped well outside the corral. Then carrying a sack of feed, I called the cows. (I had a yell that would bring them across the section.) Most of their heads came up. Then they started moving toward me. I kept shaking the 50-pound sack of feed. My purpose was to get them around me, then walk them into the compound and on into the barn.

As the cows gathered around me, another brief shower started; they pushed ever closer. I was being crowded, so I had to shove some of them out of the way before I could get to the barn. I kept up my call as they followed me inside. I also kept shaking the sack while yelling to get the guys to close the gate and not let any out. About then, I slipped in manure and mud. I went down hard, but I jumped up in a hurry so I wouldn't get trampled. Cows don't care where they step.

Once crowded inside the barn and corral, the cows tried to turn around to get back out. They were really bumping and rocking my new Cadillac, but the gate was closed. I had them exactly where I wanted them. Though they had jostled my car quite a bit, there were no dents.

Now we had to let the cattle settle a bit before we could start the next phase of the move. Once they had quieted, we removed one pickup truck and a trailer from the makeshift corral. A couple of the guys closed the gap while keeping the cattle in line by moving the portable panels closer to the cattle. Then the pickup and trailer backed up, ready to be loaded. We moved the cattle from their holding area into the trailer. That completed just the first load. It was now ready for transport to headquarters where the cattle would be fed and sheltered until going to summer pasture. That put us some time after 2 p.m.

Many loads followed, each gathered in a similar fashion, fourteen to twenty head per load. Once all the gathered cattle were on the inside of the barn, we were ready to truck more loads. Time was of the essence. Each truck-trailer combination would have to be used many times over, so we also had to figure for time to unload, gas-up, and get back to the barn.

True to his word, the farmer pulled into the far field about 4 p.m. We each continued our work until after dark. By the time we finished loading cattle, the moon was full. We were using our vehicle headlights to see what we were doing. Lastly, the bulls were loaded in three trailers. The corral panels, no longer needed, were gathered and loaded in the remaining trailer. As the last bull was being loaded in my little trailer, all the men stood by, much as you might imagine a human corral.

He was one of my favorite bulls, half buffalo, he performed well. I took many of his offspring to market: I called him Wooly Bully. As he put his front leg up into the trailer I slapped him on the butt and, as if on cue, he crapped right in my hand. It had been a long, productive day for all of us, but this was not the recognition I was looking for. The guys stood by silently observing. Then they closed the gate.

I said, "It's been that kind of day." They all started laughing. In reply, I threw the contents of my hand at them. I said, "I'm thirsty and hungry. I'm buying." We climbed into our vehicles, then headed out for the nearest café.

As we left the farm, I was last in line. I stopped to close the gate. The others continued to the café. It was only then that I realized I had been up since 4 a.m. It was now 8 p.m. Driven by a compelling purpose, I had fulfilled my agreements. My *presence* was such that I hardly noticed the passage of time. Together, we accomplished work that would normally have taken two days. From the time I arose, early in the morning, I had not eaten a thing; I had nothing to drink. Bathrooms were a forgotten luxury. None of that mattered: I was on-purpose in getting those cows moved.

You can have anything you want — if you want it badly enough.
You can be anything you want to be, do anything you set out to
accomplish if you hold to that desire with singleness of purpose.
— Abraham Lincoln[6]

When a person focuses on a clearly defined purpose, that focus and attention initiates and compels a driving force: I've been fortunate to be involved with companies where I was the first woman to work at a position previously held by a man. One position that I remember so well, and learned so much from, was being the first woman to sell ad time for WOW TV in Omaha, Nebraska. Howard Stahlnecker was the general manager. The corporate company was Meredith.
Mr. Stahlnecker brought to the industry the first Black anchor, the first woman anchor, the first woman program director, the first woman news director, and me. At the beginning of the year, he held a meeting with each department to let them know what they had accomplished in the previous year, what other stations in the market

---

[6] Abraham Lincoln, the sixteenth president of the United States

had accomplished, then what each of his own departments were expected to accomplish in the coming year. The sales manager then gave us individual goals. Guess what, we never let Mr. Stahlnecker down. If we had an idea or promotion to make the station money, his door was open and he NEVER put anyone down no matter how off-the-wall the idea seemed. He was truly loved by his people.

Mr. Stahlnecker could get everyone on-board with his purpose and that purpose would become our purpose. We learned a lot from him. With that experience behind us, we each grew into positions at larger stations, larger markets, or into other related media. All were a success in their own right.

Many people wake up each morning having no self-determined purpose in mind. Worse, some possess a purpose that has been assigned to them by someone else, a purpose that they don't particularly like. I urge my students, on the night before, to formulate a purpose and plan for the next day. Having purpose in mind, they lay out the appropriate clothes, whatever else they might need, and they are ready for work when they get up in the morning. What an asset it is for a business to have such personnel arrive each morning ready to work instead of collecting around the coffee pot trying to wake up.

Many people have a wrong idea of what constitutes true happiness. It is not attained through self-gratification, but through fidelity to a worthy purpose. – Helen Keller[7]

Having a worthy purpose applies to all aspects of life, not just business. It often amazes me that people have no purpose for their marriage. Being young and inexperienced, my first marriage revolved around having socially acceptable sex, which is to say, married sex. (It wasn't as free then as now in Modale, Iowa.)

---

[7]   Helen Keller, deafblind American author, activist, and lecturer

By my second marriage proposal, I had become a bit wiser. I dated a marvelous, loving, wealthy man for three years before he asked me to marry him. When the proposal came, I asked, "Why?"

He said he loved me, wanted to give me his name. He suggested that we could travel the world and have fun together for the rest of our lives. I said that plan would most likely last for 6 months and ruin our great friendship. So, what then will we do with the rest of our lives? We both owned our own homes, fine cars, comfortable incomes, and held station in the community. What would be a worthy, binding purpose for our marriage? He was taken aback.

Three weeks later he returned with a dynamic purpose for our marriage, one that needed two people to complete, one that would blossom with both of us involved. Most importantly to a marriage, this purpose allowed for working together the rest of our lives in something that would benefit the community. It would extend our influence well beyond the bounds of our marriage.

Presently divorce rates in the United States are holding steady at 50 percent. Perhaps if more people could assign a worthy purpose to their union that divorce rate would decline.

When a person makes known a worthy purpose, be it his or her own or another's, it seems the whole world will align in support.

Here is a test to find out whether your mission in life is complete. If you're alive, it isn't. – Richard Bach[8]

---

[8]   Richard Bach, an American writer. He is widely known as the author of the hugely popular 1970s bestsellers Jonathan Livingston Seagull, Illusions, and The Adventures of a Reluctant Messiah.

Notes:

Passion

*Don't ask yourself what the world needs; ask yourself
what makes you come alive. And then go and do that.
Because what the world needs is people who have
come alive. – Dr. Howard Thurman[9]*

In preparation for writing this chapter, I reviewed the definition
of the word passion as given in *The Century Dictionary*, last
published in 1914. Yes, I know it's an old dictionary, but it's still
a beauty in many respects. Here's a good example of how the
definition of a word can change over time.

Passion, it comes from the Latin word, *pati*, to suffer. Apparently,
as this word evolved in English it came to refer to the emotions as
distinguished from reason, usually with a negative connotation. I
suppose that could cause suffering. Using *The Century Dictionary*
as my reference, it appears that to be passionate 100 years ago
was tantamount to being out of control, like having overpowering
emotion without reason or rationale. Yet, reason without emotion
is dull, flat; it lacks oomph and accomplishment.

Passion is also defined as an intense, driving, or overmastering feeling
or conviction, even an outbreak of anger. Anger, however, could easily
amount to *passion* minus *reason* and that would not be useful to us.

---

[9] Dr. Howard Thurman, author, philosopher, theologian, educator,
civil rights leader

When I say *passion* I refer to the positive definitions found in modern dictionaries: ardent affection, love, a strong liking or desire for or devotion to some activity, object, or idea, even sexual desire would apply. For our purposes here I'll continue to use the word passion in a positive light, essentially as defined in the *American Heritage Dictionary*, an intense, driving, or overmastering feeling or conviction; a powerful emotion such as love or joy . . . Boundless enthusiasm.

Presence, *Purpose*, an intense, driving, powerful conviction, these are important tools for success that should be readily available in your life-skills toolbox.

When I recognized passion as a tool for success, I had been observing others and thinking, I've really not had a passion as I've observed in some other people, not for any of my career choices or accomplishments. I just have a continuing desire to do well, be proud of my work, and in days long gone, perhaps please Mom and Dad. When I thought of passion I always thought of such people as Robert Schuller[10] who knew when he was four-years old that he wanted to be a preacher. He planned and channeled his life to accomplish that goal. Today, he enjoys a wide sphere of influence.

Yet, I do have "boundless enthusiasm." So what is my passion?

Ah, ha! My passion is for life, study, learning, being creative, making things better for people wherever I am. When I feel the enthusiasm begin to diminish, I move on to something where I can fire that enthusiasm back up. Then I am able to use all I've learned in a new endeavor.

---

[10] The Reverend Robert Harold Schuller is an American televangelist and pastor known around the world through his weekly Hour of Power television service.

My students and clients have often asked, "What type of business should I get into? Where can I make the most money now and a few years down the road?" The best answer is obvious to me: Do what gets you fired up! Income potential is a poor substitute for something that doesn't get you fired up. Find something you can invest with your heart and soul. With such an investment, and a little bit of luck, the money will come. To do less is like trying to prosper while not being *present*.

My first husband and I moved eighteen times throughout the ten years we were married. I accepted the moves and survived by becoming proficient at finding my next job. Frequently, a job search meant starting at the bottom of any place I went to work. Wherever I went, I could secure a position; it was no big deal. Because I never had any sense of self-importance along those lines, entry level positions never bothered me. My own attitude regarding the ups and downs of life, and business, has always been quite simple: No matter what happens or where I go, I can always find work; I can always make a contribution. Unlike some people I have known, I don't let an overblown sense of pride or self-importance stand in my way. I'm willing to take an entry-level position because I know that I will be enthusiastically working my way back up yet another ladder.

On one job I went from "gofer" to vice president in two years. As a "go-fer" I started at $4,000 per year and rose to vice president at $25,000 a year. Between the vice president position and everything else I had going on, my total income was over $300,000. That was in the 1970s.

Looking for a few models of passion that everyone might recognize I turned to acting. It seems to me that Anthony Hopkins has a passion for acting.[11] His career never survived on his being the

---

[11]   Sir Philip Anthony Hopkins is a Welsh film, stage and television actor. Considered by many to be one of film's greatest living actors.

handsome, sleek, leading man who might win a part on looks first and ability second. Hopkins takes on all manner of characters, in large or small roles, good or evil, meek or otherwise. When he's acting, I believe he's the persona he portrays, not Anthony Hopkins in a different suit of clothes, mouthing his script.

Robert Duvall is another passionate actor.[12] He's earned a long career, increasingly adding to the list of characters he's played.

I enjoy watching Johnny Depp.[13] He plays characters in little or big parts. He does it well, with a passion that even in a little part, one remembers his contribution.

Meryl Streep,[14] Glenn Close,[15] and Halle Berry[16] have performed similarly in female roles.

You probably have your own favorite actors that would exemplify *passion*. You might find your own examples from different arenas and

---

[12]   Robert Selden Duvall is an Academy Award-, two-time Emmy Award-, and four-time Golden Globe Award-winning American film actor and director.

[13]   John Christopher "Johnny" Depp II is an American actor known for his portrayals of offbeat and eccentric characters. Depp has been nominated for three Academy Awards and has won Golden Globe and Screen Actors Guild Awards.

[14]   Mary Louise "Meryl" Streep is a multiple Academy Award-, Emmy-, Golden Globe-, SAG- and BAFTA Award winning American actress.

[15]   Glenn Close is an American film and stage actress and singer. Close has won an Emmy Award, three Tony Awards, and two Golden Globes; she has further been nominated for five Academy Awards, eight Emmys, and nine Golden Globes.

[16]   Halle Maria Berry is an American actress, former fashion model, and beauty queen. Berry has received Emmy and Golden Globe awards and an Academy Award for Best Actress in 2002.

occupations. I use movie actors here for example because most of us are familiar with their work. It would be a grave mistake to think anyone's life is lesser because they don't perform on Broadway, the silver screen, Carnegie Hall, or Yankee Stadium. Nearly four-hundred years ago, William Shakespeare was very right when he wrote, "All the world's a stage, and all the men and women merely players: They have their exits and their entrances; and one man in his time plays many parts . . ."

In other words, most of us have played and are playing many parts. Of those parts, some are acted out passionately, some dispassionately.

In my present work, I speak with people every day who are no more than half alive—or half dead depending on your perspective. They're perfectly normal folks, minus passion. It's my perspective that the more *presence*, *purpose*, and *passion* a person can demonstrate in his or her life, the more alive they are.

I'd like to mention a couple of real-life players on a real-life stage who impressed me many years ago:

Lee and Mary were my neighbors; they lived on a farm about a mile down the road from my first husband and me. When we met, the couple had eight children ages two to fifteen. Mary was a redheaded, Irish-Catholic with a passion for being exactly who and what she was without pretense or apology. Mary's priorities in life were simply God, Family, Church, and Community.

In most Nebraska towns there's not much to do when it comes to entertainment. There's dining at steak restaurants. Good steaks are available anywhere in Nebraska. There's drinking, dancing, card playing, going to Omaha or Sioux City for a shopping spree, more eating, more drinking, more dancing. Most people in those days did little else outside of work.

Lee was of German heritage. With his dry sense of humor, he was fun to be around. He and Mary were very affectionate all the time.

One noticeable thing was that he thanked Mary often, in different ways, for the meals, for the kids, and practically everything she contributed to the relationship and home. Believe me, she did a lot. To acknowledge themselves as a loving couple and relieve the stress of the workweek, they scheduled a night out on the town every weekend.

Farming is a rough business. Lee smoked and drank. As he struggled to make a go of the farm, he smoked and drank a lot more. Some people said that's how he lost his farm, too much drinking, but I don't know what came first, the proverbial chicken or the egg in that situation.

Lee had a heart attack when he was in his early forties. His doctor told him it would be best if he quit smoking. But, if Lee had to have a smoke, it would help to take an ounce of whiskey first to open his veins. That seemed to be when he drank much more than before.

In spite of the pressure in their lives, Lee and Mary managed a passionate relationship while holding the family together for protection, love, and companionship. When there was a problem with the children or when they were naughty, Mary never yelled as many mothers do. She used a quiet voice of reason, even with the small ones that you would think wouldn't understand the spoken word. Consequently, the children were polite, well mannered, rarely loud or out of control. Even in the spirit of play, they didn't drive a non-relative adult out of the area with their noise. Mary kept her house clean and orderly; it smelled like home because something was always cooking—mostly meat or cookies. She kept the kids clean and appropriately dressed. Cats roamed outside; the dog was always standing by for protection. Even when one of the children was diagnosed with terminal cancer, the family remained a mutually supportive unit.

I contacted Mary several years after we moved away from the area. She had twins with Lee just before he passed away. The family unit went on, driven, no doubt, by Mary's stable nurturing as well as Lee's appreciation and respect for her. Two of the older boys were in college. The ones left at home were all pitching in with the chores. Mary remarried to one of the men from their church, a man they had known for years who had been there to help during the rough times. Mary had a passion for living, loving, and in pioneer spirit, keeping on keeping on.

People do not have to be famous to have a passion for who they are and what they do. Mary proved that to me.

Editor's note: Wanda has adopted this passionate and fitting expression as her e-mail signature: "Life's journey is not to arrive at the grave safely in a well preserved body, but rather to skid in sideways, totally worn out, shouting . . . 'Holy shit what a ride!'"[17]

Notes:

---

[17] Bill McKenna, a motorcycle racer, said: "Life is not a journey to the grave with the intention of arriving safely in one pretty and well preserved piece, but to skid across the line broadside, thoroughly used up, worn out, leaking oil, shouting 'GERONIMO!'" - Cycle Magazine, February 1982

Notes:

Principles

Rules are not necessarily sacred, principles are.
– Franklin D. Roosevelt[18]

For our purposes we'll use these definitions of *principle* found in *Merriam-Webster*. They are as follows: 1. A general or fundamental law, doctrine, or assumption, 2. A rule or code of conduct, also devotion to such a code. Additionally, *The Century Dictionary* says, "Cause, in the widest sense; that by which anything is in any way ultimately determined or regulated." I find that last definition particularly interesting.

Among her other talents, my mother played piano very well. I wouldn't say she played at concert level, but at Christmas and on other occasions, she played very well. Mom wanted me to have some culture, I think, because she kept exposing me to things like piano lessons, dance, and theatre. We had a piano in the house, so I took lessons for two years. I was even in a recital. Then, my mother and my piano instructor found out that, even after all my lessons, I still couldn't read music. Perhaps you've heard the phrase, fake it until you make it? That doesn't always work.

I'd fake it by getting my teacher to play a piece so I would know how it was supposed to sound. Then, for the next week, I would just continue to repeat what I had heard until I had the piece perfected. I never even looked at the sheet music. I didn't have

---

18 Franklin D. Roosevelt, thirty-second president of the United States

to. When they figured out what I was doing, they stopped the lessons. I didn't care. I would rather be outside with the animals

than sitting in the house practicing for forty-five minutes at a time. Forty-five minutes, that's about how long I had to work at it to make my playing sound like the teacher's.

Then when I was a little older, I'm going to say around nine, Mom wanted me to have dance lessons. I don't know why she wanted that for me, but it worked out well later, having added dancing to my skill set. I might have mentioned something about dancing to Mom after seeing a movie. I really enjoyed movies, particularly ones that included dance scenes.

Here I am in costume for a dance tap recital at the Orpheum Theatre in Sioux City, Iowa. Age 11.

Mom took me to Sioux City where there was a dance studio on the second floor of a downtown building. I noticed the instructor was older than my mother, yet she had a great body with very muscular legs. She taught tap, ballet, and toe. She could perform each of these styles, and perform them fascinatingly well.

Mom committed to a month's worth of lessons every Saturday at 11 a.m. She told me that I would have to commit to practice just like I had for the piano. If I was proficient enough, I would be in a recital at the Orpheum Theatre. That was a big deal to me because that theatre hosted road shows with stars that I would see in the movies.[19]

My parents would put me on a bus in Walthill. I walked from the bus terminal to the dance studio. That would have been about five blocks from the terminal. (Just south of the studio there was a hotdog and hamburger grill. They always had thirty or more dogs on the grill in the window and they were so good. That may have been part of the attraction to dancing. Ha)

I showed a great deal of persistence with dance. I worked and reworked my dance steps with attention to certain movements of the body, or no movements depending on which steps I was doing. Then, expanding on my personal skills, I practiced working with others doing the same routines. We practiced until the sounds and rhythms of our shoes were like that of one person. Admittedly, I was not graceful enough for ballet, but I learned some of the ballet moves by watching others. I had plenty of opportunity as the ballet class ended right before mine would start up. Our class studied tap. Following the tap class, there was a woman who received private lessons on toe technique. She was so beautiful and graceful that I frequently hung around to watch, captivated by her presence and motion. The instructor often had to remind me that I had a bus to catch.

One time I left the studio without being reminded. I walked to the bus station arriving a little early. There I walked around looking for something to read. One of my favorite hangouts was a magazine stand where I found a publication that had the words to all the popular songs of the time. It was there that I spotted a book that I couldn't ignore, *The 7 Great Religions of the World*. That was the first time I took a conscious risk: I looked at that book.

---

[19] The Orpheum hosted many popular entertainers, among them Fred Astaire, Tallulah Bankhead, and Katherine Hepburn.

After a year of indoctrination in Catholic School and catechism, I just knew if I read that book I would be risking my immortal soul. What would the nuns say? My burning desire mixed with these counter-considerations presented me with a really serious dilemma. I sat and looked at that book for at least fifteen minutes, maybe twenty. Finally, I thought I could, perhaps, absolve myself by doing a penance of some kind. I reasoned that I had the rest of my life to do it, so I bought the book. I started reading it right away.

I read it on the bus ride back home. I put it away when Mom picked me up at the station. During our drive, we talked about dance class. I told her there was an upcoming recital. There might be some extra practices I would have to attend. I needed a costume. She would have to make it. I would be doing a sailor dance. It would be fun as it was a march, one of my favorites. I might have a starring roll with a black kid who could dance really well. He could do splits and other unusual moves. I just didn't think I could keep up with him.

As I voiced my considerations, Mom encouraged me; she was certain I could keep up. She felt that I probably had to do some extra practice, but I would do fine. She let me know that if I needed an extra lesson or two, she and Dad would work it out.

At home that night I overheard them talking; Mom was telling Dad about the recital; I might need extra money for lessons. Although we were in the planting season and money was tight, Dad said, "Whatever she needs, I'll just make more money."

(I heard that attitude expressed a number of times while I was in their care.)

While Mom and Dad were talking, I was upstairs in my room reading my new book. Wow, I couldn't put it down. I held in my hands a great deal of information, new perspectives to pique my interests. I read it whenever I had the time.

I began thinking, I often heard the elders of the Omaha Tribe drumming in the evening, but it had never occurred to me that the drumming was part of their religious practice. I was only aware of one aspect of their religious lives, that they went to a Christian Church. So, as my perspectives changed, I imagined people could be pliable in their religious practices, too. Why not?

My folks never questioned how I spent the money they gave me. So there was no explaining that I had spent money on the book. Although Mom must have suspected, as mothers do, that I had a new interest, as I did spend more time in my room that week reading.

By the next Saturday morning I had finished the book. Before the bus ride to practice I came downstairs for breakfast. I placed the book on the kitchen table, face up. Mom was busy cooking. She glanced over at the book to read the title. She asked me what I thought of it.

I said, "It's interesting that all the religions seem to have a man with a message that started a movement. Then there was usually a book. Often he is put to death. They all believe in a special place one goes after death. They believe in giving to their religion, money or something that is important. They think you should help your neighbor and that you're a spirit of some kind. They are all so similar to me. Zoraster's seems to be the story of Jesus, but before. It really makes you think and wonder."

Mom had an amusing, little smile when she knew that I was using my head for something besides a hat rack. She was proud, I think, but never said much only, "That's very wise of you. Now just continue to believe that and treat everyone as you would like to be treated."

Throughout my life I found for myself that this motherly advice is a basic principle of the Universe. Making this principle my own has brought me good health, above average wealth, and great happiness.

Now late in my life as I reflect on Mom, I see this highly educated woman married to a man with a fifth-grade education. She was well trained in her profession, competent in her life, yet she never pushed me to be anyone or anything but me. My mother exposed, taught, and drilled me in those things that I naturally found interesting. She taught me principles that I use to this day, and she allowed me to develop my own principles, too. I know she could have gone anywhere, done anything, and accomplished more in her allotted time on this earth, but she chose to be with Dad and me. She taught me a lot by the example she set, her obvious commitment to the people and things she loved, and her unwavering perseverance. That's quite a gift.

As always, Dad made the extra money we needed. I had my extra dance lessons. I was in a group dance, but I also did a partner dance with the black boy. He was *so* good. I guess I must have been "okay" since I was the one selected to dance with him. Mom and Dad were both in the audience that night. Some experiences a person just doesn't forget.

A few years later I took my dancing skills into ice-skating and roller-skating. There I made a success of those activities, particularly the ice-skating. All the while I used the information I gleaned from that book on religion, carrying it with me into this day. I watched my parents interact, how they worked as a team. Now I can say that they likely shared many similar principles. That would be part of the "secret" to having a successful marriage.

Mom had her books, music, and she enjoyed keeping up with current events. There were plays in Omaha that we attended together. I still enjoy remembering the late evenings driving home where we would chat about our experience at the show while enjoying the ride.

As I look back now, that moment at the book and magazine stand is when I decided to step out of the box people were creating for me. I decided to be my own person. In my indoctrinated mind, to step out like that was taking a huge risk with my immortal soul–but I really wanted to know more about life and religion.

Any one of us is being guided through life by principles gleaned from such varied sources as parents, church, school, literature, movies, and so on. We even formulate our own principles along the way, some being workable, and some not so workable.

Some principles are obvious and easily accepted when they appear. Some rest quietly in the background of the mind until fully understood. Some are remembered when the life situation calls for it, others are forgotten. Here's a principle that must have been obvious to the person who stated it, but was probably forgotten later in his life: "When things go wrong don't go with them." Elvis Presley the American pop icon said that. It seems to be sound advice. Perhaps he was just being clever in the moment. Perhaps he was just parroting someone else. I really don't know.

Here's a principle about principles that might have guided Abraham Lincoln, the sixteenth president of the United States, through his country's civil war: He said, "Important principles may and must be inflexible." Pliability, being flexible, is one of my nine power tools for success, but important, overarching principles are constant.

Joseph Wood Krutch, an American writer, critic, and naturalist stated, "Cats seem to go on the principle that it never does any harm to ask for what you want." That one would apply to people as well. It doesn't do any harm to ask for what you want. If you don't ask, you might never receive. One of the mistakes that apprentice salespeople make after all their hard work of prospecting, contacting, and showing the product is, they forget to ask for the sale.

Examples of principles tossed around our culture are many. Children should be seen and not heard. That's a dated cliché, but at times still very applicable. The context to which the principle is applied is also important.

"It takes more courage to reveal insecurities than to hide them, more strength to relate to people than to dominate them, more 'manhood' to abide by thought-out principles rather than blind reflex. Toughness is in the soul and spirit, not in muscles and an immature mind." Alex Karras, the former football player, professional wrestler, and actor said that. Good for you Alex! I personally don't know Alex Karras, but I would bet he had to review some youthful, rough and tumble, self-absorbed principles accumulated while playing football and wrestling before he could take full ownership of the mature statement above.

It would be common to find a person holding onto one or more principles in conflict. This mental state tends to zap a person's personal power and eventually their physical energy. In extreme cases, productivity will suffer, as will joy and passion for living. It's an uncommon person who knows exactly who he or she is, possessed of clearly defined goals and purposes. One of the most common examples I can think of where a person is likely to be struggling with conflicting principles is post traumatic stress disorder (PTSD) suffered by returning soldiers. As civilians and honorable beings they probably subscribe to the principle that, "Thou shalt not kill," and who as soldiers must kill an assigned enemy.

Speaking of toughness of soul and spirit and treating others as you would like to be treated, perhaps a person would need to begin exercising this principle by consciously setting the example. If they teach it to their family, if they are an example to their friends and coworkers, etc., they will begin to have positive things happen, life will change for the better.

Another basic principle I have involves maintaining a positive attitude. If I fall or get knocked down, I pick myself back up. I don't choose a bad attitude, then stay down grumbling about my situation. Yes, attitude for a self-determined person is a choice.

My mother often said to me, "Wanda, you're as good as everyone and everyone is as good as you no matter their color, creed or occupation. When you work for someone, work hard enough that it will take him or her five minutes to replace you. Most people can be replaced in a minute."

There you have a couple of my adopted principals along with a few other examples I rounded up from various sources. Although I was programmed with certain principles by my mother, I've looked them over, then decided to keep them as my own. Now I know that times have changed, people don't necessarily think that way anymore, but those principles have worked for me.

One of my dad's principles that I've decided to keep is, "Once you give your word, be responsible. Keep your word no matter how much it costs you in time, money, or energy." He stated this principle in a number of different ways, but always intending what he meant, and meaning what he said. Applying this principle to my own life has cost me a couple hundred-thousand dollars. As a result, I've had some serious, personal coaching on this matter. Generally, it's still a good principle, but now I am apt to look carefully before I give *my word*. Moreover, I've been known to take that commitment back when warranted, most often on my former husband. I've decided "former" sounds better than "ex." I think that would be a good national cause, let's call all of them "ex's" simply "formers."

When you read the principles (tenets, precepts) of many of the world's religions, you'll find such basic principles as "treat your neighbor as well as you would like to be treated." In that regard, the world's religions have much in common. My own version is, treat your neighbor at least ten times as well as you'd like to be treated. That way I feel secure in the knowledge that I am upholding the principle.

I think it's a good business practice to treat customers, employees, and employers as I, myself, would like to be treated. If this were the norm in our society, I venture to say there would be many more equitable deals being arranged and kept; business would flow more smoothly. I can only imagine how that might affect living standards and the world economy. Am I going out too far on a limb to say that fairness and equity seem to be lacking today? Maybe I am. Yet, if we start practicing some of these old principles close to home with my business and your business, I promise you, our businesses will overcome any recession and begin to boom. I guess that philosophy has a lot to do with my positive attitude, too.

Let's face it, it's easy to talk of ourselves as having principles while perceiving that others do not. It's a big step forward to move from talk to putting said principles into practice. I am aware that some spouses talk to each other in public with an attitude and verbiage that isn't civil, much less polite, kind, or considerate. When I see these people, I wonder what they were like with each other on their first date? What changed since then? Why can't they treat each other at least as they would like to be treated? Would the divorce rate diminish? Also, isn't it about time that we treat our children with kindness, consideration, and thought as when we first saw them as infants?

Since I am in the mood, let's make a deal: For one day, I challenge you to shut off the radio, TV, cable, and video games. I mean OFF! For that one day, I challenge you be especially kind and considerate. It's a challenge to appreciate everyone, every act that anyone does no matter how difficult it may be. It's going to be hard. Even if the act is negative or evil, find a way to make it positive in your mind. I promise you, this exercise will bring you joy, a really good feeling about yourself. After all, YOU are the most important being in your universe. Your observations, communications, and contributions to others amount to something unique. Never forget it.

It was Benjamin Franklin who stated, "If principle is good for anything, it is worth living up to." I would agree.

The Hindu Prince Gautama Siddharta, the founder of Buddhism, is reported to have said, "All that we are is the result of what we have thought. The mind is everything. What we think, we become."

Also, here's a reminder of the definition of principle: "Cause, in the widest sense; that by which anything is in any way ultimately determined or regulated."

If it's true that we are what we think, if it's true that what we think is Cause, wouldn't it be wise to review one's principles, then let go of the ones that no longer apply, and focus on the ones that do?

Presence, Purpose, Passion, Principles: Expect a miracle! It could happen!

Notes:

Promises

Promise little and do much. – Hebrew Proverb

The *American Heritage Dictionary* defines *promise*:

Noun: 1a. A declaration assuring that one will or will not do something; a vow, b. Something promised, 2. Indication of something favorable to come; expectation: a promise of spring in the air, 3. Indication of future excellence or success: a player of great *promise*.

Transitive verb: 1. To commit oneself by a promise to do or give; pledge: left but promised to return, 2. To afford a basis for expecting: thunderclouds that promise rain.

Intransitive verb: 1. To make a declaration assuring that something will or will not be done, 2. To afford a basis for expectation: *an enterprise that promises well.*

Promises are the way we work with each other placing order and predictability into the future. A bona fide *promise* says, "This you can count on."

My dad, never satisfied with being stuck with the limitations of being just a farmer, was always looking for ways to make money. He farmed for a living, but he really loved the adventure of trading. The day he died, he and I were in the middle of negotiating a sale of thirty-eight Shetland ponies. At the time, he wanted me to take these ponies to one of the largest horse sales on the High Plains.

From the time I was a baby, Dad fed cattle, bought hundreds of boar hogs, castrated them, fed them until they healed, then sold them as fat hogs. Dad fed calves, cows, steers, heifers, and goats with the expectation of taking them all to market. He bought workhorses, then sold them to packing plants for dog food. He even sent some of the horses to Europe where horse meat is an acceptable source of protein. Always wheeling and dealing, Dad bought animals direct from farmers, sale barns, and stockyards.

Dad used to say he didn't want to put all his eggs in one basket, "Cause if one egg goes bad, all the other eggs in the basket might go bad with it, so you end up with nothing; but if you have several eggs in several baskets, one or more can give you an income." Putting all of one's eggs in one basket is an idiom, an old piece of popular folk philosophy, used so much it's now a cliché. Nevertheless, it's still good advice. Just ask anyone who has lost a bundle in a downturning stock market.

Not surprisingly, the one time I lost all my money was when I failed to heed Dad's wisdom. I put everything in one basket, so to speak.

Anyhow, at this particular time, he was farrowing sows.[20] As for me, I would hang out with Dad and Grandpa every chance I had.

One sow had twelve piglets, but one was so small and weak that they were discussing putting him out of his misery. As is common with the runt of the litter, he didn't have a chance competing with the other, stronger piglets. I begged Dad and Grandpa to let me have it. I *promised* I'd try to be its "mom."

---

[20] Farrowing, giving birth to piglets

Dad told me this would be a commitment for several months. He told me I would have to care for it, feed it, keep it safe, make a place for it, and otherwise be totally responsible for it.

I said, "Oh, yes Daddy, I promise!"

The first two weeks were really hard on me. Fortunately, it was summer and school was out. I fed "Spotty" before I ate in the morning, then at noon, again at night and, finally, before I went to bed.

I took to caring for the piglet as any little girl might care for any baby animal: I loved and nurtured him thereby turning him into a pet. I was able to put Spotty in the brooder house as the chicks were grown and in the chicken yard. I would take him outside in the daytime. I'd lay with him so he could pick up the heat from the sun while my body would shield him from the wind. I put Spotty in my doll buggy. In that way I could take him with me wherever I would go. I would also carry him wrapped in a doll blanket. We went everywhere together, so everyone who knew me also knew Spotty.

There was one exception to Spotty traveling with me everywhere I went: There was no bringing Spotty into the house. None of my animals were allowed in the house, not the dog, the cat, the chickens, none. The house was for people only.

The pig lived well in my care. He grew. I taught it tricks. Spotty would even do tricks that the dog wouldn't do. He would climb a ladder joining me on the roof of the house. Getting him down was the real trick. I usually just carried him down the ladder. Spotty would ride in my wagon. I also had a horse and buggy. Spotty would ride in the buggy sitting or laying down. He followed me everywhere. If I walked to Grandpa's house, the barn, downtown, wherever I went he'd follow. Furthermore, my dog and Spotty became buddies.

Flowers would not grow in the dirt around our house. My mom tried very hard, but the land just would not support plant life. With much hard work, she eventually developed and nurtured a beautiful bed of moss roses. They grew along the south side of the house. It was a major achievement when the flower bed was finally lush with blossoms of various colors.

By now Spotty was good-sized, twice as big as my bulldog. All along I had treated him essentially like another dog. He'd sleep all night by the back door with the dog. When it came to Spotty's bathroom needs, he had his own place to go. Believe it or not, hogs choose their own bathroom; that's where they go all the time. I fed him every morning and evening.

An acre of performance is worth a whole world of promise.
– William Dean Howells[21]

One day while I was eating a late breakfast, Mom went to the pump to fill her bucket with water. She had no sooner left the house than I heard her call my name loud and clear. I ran outside. My eyes followed Mom's gaze and her pointing finger.

There sat Spotty in the middle of the flower bed, flowers hanging out of each side of his mouth, and a couple on the top of his head where he had rooted. Golly, it was hilarious, but I didn't dare laugh. At that moment even the dog was afraid, and he was behind me!

With presence, principles, and passion, Mom told me to, "Get that animal where he belongs with the other hogs: Now!" She informed me that I had not kept my promise to care for the pig.

---

[21] William Dean Howells was an American realist author and literary critic.

"Care for" meant more than just feeding it. "Care for" meant, "Keep it out of the way!"

So, I called Spotty. He slowly followed me out the back yard gate, across the pasture, through the gate to the hog lot. When I arrived there Dad asked me what happened. I told him. I also said I didn't think that it was fair, I had taken care of him.

Dad reminded me that he had told me a couple of times that it was time for Spotty to go in the feedlot with the other pigs. He reminded me of my promise to look after him. I knew what a trip to the feedlot meant. It meant going to the market to be butchered.

Don't fall in love with the animals. They have a purpose and it usually involves their death. — Grandpa French

Reluctantly, I left Spotty in the feedlot. I hugged him, then told him I'd come play with him. He went to the trough to eat. Dad and the hired man went on feeding all the other animals. He and the hired man milked the cows while I went by Grandpa's house to see if there was something good to eat there.

When I returned home, Mom was not happy. To my chagrin, Spotty had returned to the house ahead of me. We had steps that went over the fence in all the yards. Spotty simply had his breakfast, then walked over the steps to beat me back home. I thought he was lucky that Mom didn't butcher him on the spot!

When I took him back to the feedlot, Dad said he didn't think it would be a good idea for me to come visit him any more. I should, perhaps, stay with Spotty only until Dad finished milking the cow. Dad acknowledged that I had done a very good job keeping my word when Spotty was a baby. Dad also stressed that he should have been firmer about putting Spotty back with the other hogs sooner. It was my responsibility to feed him and keep him fenced. He also reminded me that life is not always fair.

Dad went on to explain that the matter of taking care of the pig was not for just a few weeks, or only as long as it held my interest, but for the entire time the animal was on the farm. Dad advised me that a person should never get as close to a farm animal as I had, not to any animal that was raised for market purposes. During the talk, he also complemented my persistence. He recognized my hard work ensuring the pig would live. An extra hog to market meant a lot to the family income.

The next time Dad loaded hogs to go to market he told me he didn't need my help. He said I should stay in the house. However, I left the house telling Mom I was going to watch. I watched them loading Spotty along with fifty to sixty other hogs. At that point, I just shrank into a state of no-presence. I wanted to become invisible. I turned and ran home. There I sat hugging my dog until the moon came up. When Dad returned from loading the hogs, he told me it was time to come in and go to bed.

For every promise, there is price to pay. – Jim Rohn[22]

Three years later I took to feeding calves for my 4-H[23] project. Again, I promised Dad I would take care of the calves. This time

---

[22] Jim Rohn is an American entrepreneur, author, and motivational speaker.

[23] 4-H in the United States is a youth organization administered by the Dept. of Agriculture. The four "H's" stand for Head, Heart, Hands, and Health. The goal of 4-H is to develop citizenship, leadership, and life skills of youth through mostly experiential learning programs. Though typically thought of as an agriculturally focused organization as a result of its history, 4-H today focuses on citizenship, healthy living, and science, engineering and technology programs.

I did. I was completely responsible spending many, many hours gentling them, getting them to trust and obey me. I fed them, washed them, dried them, curried them. I lived up to my word. When my champion calves were sold at auction after the big show, I had earned a huge profit. Keeping my promise, I took the show halter off of them, turned, then walked away with no emotional connection.

These are my 4-H show champions. "Joe," a shorthorn standing next to me was Grand Champion. "Buss" stood behind him. The picture was taken in one of our feedlots on the farm. Dad is squatted by Buss near his front legs as I couldn't reach the lead on his halter. Joe is the one that went to Sioux City for a red ribbon and Buss is the one that went to Omaha and then on to show at the Cow Palace in San Francisco. Buss was one of the first, if not the first, crossbred calf to show at a major event in the area. The calf was Blue. His mother was a Black Angus and his father a White Shorthorn. Buss weighed 1265 pounds when he was sold. Joe weighed 1140 three weeks earlier.

I was ten when the calves were sold. I had in my name over $5,000 in the bank. My folks never asked me for anything. However, I realized that Dad initially bought the calves. I fed his corn to them. It seemed only right that he should see a return on the investment. So, for Christmas I gave Mom a Christmas card with a check for $2,000. I gave another $2,000 check to Dad in his Christmas card. I kept the rest to buy them anniversary presents in January, then birthday presents for each of them in March. When the calves were sold, and after I had satisfied my self-imposed obligations, I bought myself a Springer Spaniel hunting dog, a .410 shotgun, and three government savings bonds.

This is the point I wish to make: All of us need to have or develop a keen awareness of how very, very important it is to keep one's promises. In my opinion, keeping one's promises is a way of paying forward on goodwill, trust, and confidence. It is part of the essence that holds our civilized society together. In my experience, the universe around me has rewarded me often for keeping my promises, often in the most unexpected ways.

The things here that I am calling rewards might be recognized by some people as miracles or gifts from God. However you wish to understand these phenomena, I would ask that you be present, allow the Universe to deliver assistance, guidance, or whatever you need or want. Perhaps a particular person will come into your life at just the right time, to fill a void, to assist in your business plan, or to marry. Perhaps something like a song or a few words of good will are just what you need to set you off in a positive direction. Perhaps a jog around the block, a walk on the beach, or a rain storm will put you in a mental place where you are now able to see solutions where, before, there were only difficulties. Perhaps ideas or material things will come your way to complete an invention you have been trying to complete. Perhaps this very book is exactly what you need at this time.

Perhaps you've heard the expression, what goes around comes around? I think there's a great deal of truth in it. Therefore, I don't concern myself with broken promises. If someone breaks a promise too often, or breaks a really big promise, it destroys their credibility with me. I just find a new partner or associate. I do business elsewhere. My promises to others are the important ones. These promises I can control; they go around and come around.

In my business experience, keeping promises helps the business grow financially; it earns recognition in the community, and much more. Pay salaries to your employees on time with good funds. Send payable checks out to creditors when due, along with mortgages, bank notes, etc. Prompt, reliable payment builds character and credibility. Occasionally, times may prove tough. One will need a little help just to get through. By paying forward as mentioned above, help is there for you many times when you think there is no way out.

In relationships, if you learn to keep your promise to your spouse and children, they all know you say what you mean and mean what you say. They know that a promise made will be kept to them. Be it discipline or praise, it will happen as you've promised.

When one has a reputation of keeping a promise, the Universe will provide what is needed and wanted. You don't believe me? Just try it! It would do many people some good to take a personal inventory of promises made then kept as well as promises made then broken. Clean up the past by looking over broken promises and other upsets, let go of them, then prepare to move forward.

Promises kept is another, vital, personal power tool to be used in all areas of life, for health, wealth, and happiness.

Notes:

Persistence

Fall seven times, stand up eight. – Japanese Proverb

If we are facing in the right direction,
all we have to do is keep on walking. – Buddhist Saying

Merriam–Webster defines *persist* as: 1. to go on resolutely or stubbornly in spite of opposition, importunity, or warning, 2. obsolete: to remain unchanged or fixed in a specified character, condition, or position, 3. to be insistent in the repetition or pressing of an utterance (as a question or an opinion), 4. to continue to exist especially past a usual, expected, or normal time.

Persistence: 1. To go on resolutely or stubbornly in spite of difficulties, 2. To continue to exist.

For many of us, our most personal and relevant experience with persistence has been when we've been in competition. When I was ten, I was among other children in the area who raised calves for 4-H. I was in competition with older kids, mostly boys. I should mention, Dad raised me like he would have raised the boy he didn't have. I was expected to perform better than the boys.

Later in my life, I would compete with the "boys" on their grownup playing fields in sales, ranching, trading, etc. My early experience in 4-H was a perfect setup. There I learned that I can compete with anyone, being no less than an equal. I learned that I can win. I learned how it feels to be handsomely rewarded for a job well done.

Every day, in the summer months, before the county fair, I washed, combed, and walked the calves. I followed that routine by putting them through show positions. There was no one hanging over my shoulder saying, "It's time for you to go take care of your calves." The work was expected, as I gave my word that I would do what was needed to win.

Skating on rollers in summer when there was no ice.

Every day for hours upon hours, I worked with the calves. My calves and I won Grand Champion, Reserve Champion, and fifth place in Top 6 of the county. From there we went on to the regional shows where we won blue ribbons. The hardest thing for me about the whole discipline was knowing that in the end these pals would be slaughtered and, worst yet, the Grand Champion was bought by the county fathers to be the meat served up at the 4-H Banquet! I didn't eat much that night!

A few years later I became interested in figure skating. Raising the calves proved to be an excellent introduction to discipline and persistence. We lived fifty miles from the nearest rink. Every Friday after school my mother put me on a bus to Omaha. From 5 p.m. Friday until Sunday at 9 p.m. I skated thirty hours in class, in private lessons, and session time. I repeated figures, jumps, spins, and footwork for hours.

The first lesson taught me how to fall. So, I knew from the beginning that I would be falling and that I might be hurt. One does fall a lot: get up, fall, get up, fall, get up, fall, get up . . . I practiced and performed hundreds, perhaps thousands, of sit-spins. As a result, I developed strength in the muscles below my knees that even most men never develop.

Later in life when farming, I learned that one plants the corn, eliminates weeds, insects and varmints, picks, then dries the corn. Market prices can fluctuate widely by the time a crop is ready, so one accepts whatever price the market offers at the time of delivery. If a flood or hail should wipe you out, you replant, then at the end of the year you start all over. That's persistence!

Perhaps you've heard the old joke: A stranger to New York City stops his cab to ask for directions, "Hey kid, how do you get to Carnegie Hall?"

The kid says, "Practice, Mister, Practice!"

Practice, practice, practice, that's persistence in attaining a skill.

Farmers, ranchers, artisans, athletes, artists, writers, dancers, actors, each reach performance levels because they practice, practice, practice. It's not just practice per se as practice with bad form leads to bad performance. It's persistence with ever increasing knowledge and skill toward a known goal or objective; that's what makes a winner! Persisting with inadequate knowledge, help, or skill just makes one appear to be stubborn; that's not always a good thing.

> *With ordinary talent and extraordinary perseverance, all*
> *things are attainable. – Sir Thomas Foxwell Buxton*

If it is not yet apparent, I should mention that the successful events in my life—perhaps anyone's life—are occasioned by most, if not all, of the nine power tools: *Presence, Purpose, Passion, Principles, Promises, Persistence, Parters, Pliability, Planning.*

Now I'd like to tell you about my dear, persistent friend, Pat Nolan. In my estimation, this woman is the best copywriter in all of Omaha. To compliment her professional talent, she possesses remarkable persistence. I observed this trait demonstrated in her work. When it came time to play, Pat was equally persistent.

For years, Pat encouraged me to join the organization, American Women in Radio and Television (AWRT). While I managed to thwart this particular desire of hers, Pat was able to pull me into other adventures that never would have crossed my mind: white water rafting on the Colorado River, volunteer work in the bowels of the Omaha Orpheum Theatre during opera season, etc.

In 1970, Pat was on my case again to join AWRT. AWRT was having their first international conference in London. Airfares were reasonably priced. A stay in a London Hotel was very affordable. The entire trip would be inexpensive, and fun, too! The only catch was, I had to become a member of AWRT. So I joined.

We arrived in London early in the morning. Our room at the Royal Garden wasn't ready, so we walked around London for about four hours. Once we were able to get into our rooms, we took a brief nap. Then we registered for the convention.

I believe that in those days, most women in England were teachers, nurses, hair dressers, nannies, secretaries, and so on. Not many were entrepreneurial or held executive positions. I'd say most of the women of AWRT, if not all, were powerful women. That made this group of one-thousand women somewhat unique.

The conference organizers kept us scheduled beginning at 8 a.m. They kept us busy right until midnight. After midnight, host rooms were setup for socializing. AWRT members were expected to attend all meals as notable speakers were present, including the president of the BBC, and the presidents of ABC, NBC, and CBS. In addition, we toured the city to see many of the highlights: London Tower, the House of Commons, the House of Lords, china manufacturing facilities, etc.

By the way, the royal jewels are just fabulous! Unbelievable! Have you ever seen a diamond that was over 3,000 carats!

The conference organizers also kept us entertained in the early evenings by introductions to theatre, movie, and TV people.

About the third day of the conference, some the women of AWRT were invited to Lancaster House for cocktails with Princess Margaret.

When we arrived, we were ushered into a beautiful reception room. It was regal—stunning to say the least.

The crown molding was hand carved with scrolls, delicate and magnificent, covered in gold leaf. The chandeliers were leaded crystal, clean and sparkly as if they had just been polished. The carpet was thick wool with an antique look. I'm certain it was old, but it looked new. Even the door knobs looked like they were real gold.

In back of us, tables were setup with Champagne glasses and delicate finger food. Waiters dressed in black and white stood ready to serve.

We were briefed by a lady-in-waiting. She instructed us to speak with Her Majesty only if she spoke to us first. We were instructed on how to drop the head, lower the eyes, and give a small curtsy, maybe a six-inch dip. The lady-in-waiting showed us where to position ourselves in line allowing Princess Margaret an efficient stroll from the entry door to the exit door, both doors being on the same wall. I'm guessing there were maybe fifty of us in that room. Princess Margaret would enter the room, make her way down the U-shaped line of us women, then exit.

We were in our places when the door opened. A herald wearing a mid-1700s costume walked in: triangle-shaped hat, a shirt with a bow that tied at the neck, white socks to the knees, trousers that blossomed over the top of his socks, shoes with large buckles, a heavy coat with wide cuffs that was flared at the waist. He carried a long, metal septre with a big ball on the top. It looked heavy and sounded heavy when he hit it on the floor which he did to announce all the events, including breakfast, lunch, and dinner.

The herald knocked his septre three times on the floor and announced, "Her Royal Highness, The Princess Margaret, Countess of Snowdon."

Then he announced, "His Royal Highness, The Prince Charles Philip Arthur George, Prince of Wales and Earl of Chester."

Some women did, "Oh or Awe" over Prince Charles' names, but then quieted. The two royals stepped ever so quietly in the room. All present were quiet. Princess Margaret started down the row, welcoming and thanking people for coming to London.

After the royals left the room, we were served Champagne.

The next night, theatre, TV, and movie people entertained us in Guild Hall. The cast of *Hair*, *The Avengers*, and movie people were there. During the evening, I spoke with Lynn Redgrave, Omar Sharif, and the cast of *The Avengers*. I don't know why, but a movie scriptwriter was so fascinated with me that he insisted I meet his mother and father, Lord and Lady (somebody) who were at the event.

At the end of the day, Pat and I left our fine clothes in storage at the Royal Garden Hotel. We left Victoria Station on the boat train making Paris our next stop on our two-week, European adventure.

Pat and I carried the book, *Europe On $5 a Day* as our guide. That five-dollars must be at least fifty dollars a day now. Due to some political unrest at the time, we heard that the French tended to not like Americans, so we made up our minds that no matter how impolite people might be with us, we would be polite with them. We also decided that I would handle our money since Pat had trouble figuring exchange rates. We planned to split up each day, then meet at the hotel that night to discuss our adventures over dinner. That way we wouldn't get on each others nerves by being in constant contact. Most importantly, we'd still be friends at the end of the trip. It was a good plan.

Pat and I spent five days in Paris having super-fun adventures. (I'll have to save telling about those for another book.) Then we left for Rome on the Palatino Train.

Each time we went to a new city, we would first take a tour on a Panorama Tour Bus. After the bus tour, Pat and I would return to the places where we wanted to spend more time. In Rome, the tour bus took us to the edge of town, close to the Spanish Steps, then ended up at the Vatican around lunch time. The beauty, statues, wood, marble, paintings, gold, everything to pique the senses, would take anyone's breath away. In our awestruck wandering, we missed our bus ride. We didn't care.

At the Vatican, I spotted a group of about thirty people collected in a small alcove of the church. I wondered what was going on, so I searched for someone to speak with. I finally found a man who spoke English. He told me the people were waiting for a blessing from the Pope (Paul VI).

I said to Pat, "Come on, let's go see the Pope."

Pat said, "We can't do that. We don't have an invitation."

I said, "Come on. What can they do? Throw us out? Let's go!"

We casually walked over, then joined the group. No one seemed to mind. We made our way to the railing where we would receive our blessings. Still no one seemed to mind. I looked around. The lighting was obviously orchestrated to present the Pope in the best light. He came out from behind an alter. He appeared to be floating. The illusion was no doubt due to the lighting, his robes, and his smooth walk.

The Pope was of slight build. His robes looked weighty on his small frame. He walked from one end of the group to the other. He blessed all of us while making the sign of the cross. I readily received his blessing because, most of the time, I need all the blessings I can get.

The presentation was perfect. The marketing and sales person in me relished the experience. I was close enough to reach out and touch him. The Pope was systematically doing his job; he blessed everyone. He made no special effort to connect with anyone excepting a man that seemed to be the leader of the people who waited in the alcove. They spoke with each other for a few minutes. Pat and I gently backed off, then left the area.

In 1974, I became president of the local chapter of AWRT, you know, that organization I didn't want to join just a few years earlier. There, among other accomplishments, I started a fund-raising program to assist hospitalized children.

Just think, if Pat hadn't been her persistent self, I would have missed one of the great adventures of my life. Thanks Pat!

Partners

I try to work with God as a partner. – Gary Player[24]

The *American Heritage Dictionary of the English Language*: defines *partner* thus: Noun: 1. One that is united or associated with another or others in an activity or a sphere of common interest, especially: a. A member of a business partnership, b. A spouse, c. A domestic *partner*, d. Either of two persons dancing together, e. One of a pair or team in a sport or game, such as tennis or bridge.

Transitive verb: 1. To make a partner of, 2. To bring together as partners, 3. To be the partner of.

Intransitive verb: To work or perform as a partner or partners.

Parents:

Few if any of us ever make great strides in life without forming a number of special partnerships. I mentioned several times how I won the 4-H competition with my champion calves. In all fairness, I should tell you about some of the support I received from my parents, parents who were also silent partners in my success. Even though I was caring for the animals by myself, Dad was instrumental in my training and overall management of when, where, and how the calves would be presented.

---

[24] Gary Player, professional golfer generally regarded as one of the greatest players in the history of the game.

The county 4-H competition took place in August. Beyond the 4-H competitions, there were larger, regional livestock shows, usually open to the county 4-H Grand Champion and Reserve Champion calves. Dad decided we would take the Grand Champion to the big show in Sioux City. That show would be in September, three weeks after the county show. Larger cattle were favored in Sioux City. With three more weeks of added weight, we expected our Grand Champion to do well. Dad thought our Reserve Champion would perform best at the Ak-Sar-Ben (Omaha) stock show, three weeks after the Sioux City show.[25]

There was an elimination process at each show. We made it past that part of the competition. In Sioux City, my Grand Champion received a red ribbon; that's second place.

For some reason unbeknownst to me, both Mom and Dad couldn't stay in Sioux City the night before the auction. They checked out of the hotel where the three of us had been staying. I stayed behind. My duty would be taking care of the calves in the evening and, again, the next morning before the auction. Dad would do his best to be back in Sioux City before the auction started.

Before Mom and Dad left Sioux City, Dad coached me on how the auction process worked. I would feed the calves at night, but not the next morning. They could have water until 7 a.m., nothing after that.

The auction would start at 1 p.m. The calves would be weighed going out of the auction just like at the sale barn at home. I was familiar with auctions at the sale barn. I could feed the calves as much as they wanted in the evening, then I had to be there at 6 a.m. for their one, allowed drink. I could wash and groom the calves for the remainder of the morning.

---

[25] Ak-Sar-Ben is Nebraska spelled backwards.

My folks left the auction barn about 4 p.m the afternoon before the auction. I would be alone that night, in my room at the hotel. They always gave me plenty of money, so that was never a problem. I fed the calves. While they were eating, I decided to take a walk around the show. I saw a man selling giant bags of popcorn. I love popcorn; it's my favorite snack. I bought a bag, then I went back to the calves. I pulled up a bale of hay placing it against the partition between the rows of calves. I sat down with my popcorn.

My calves came to me. It turned out they were attracted by the popcorn. I gave them some; they scarfed it down. It occurred to me, the salt on the popcorn might make them thirsty; they would drink more water thus adding weight.

I went back to the vendor and bought ten bags of popcorn. He asked me what I was doing with all the corn. I said, "My friends really like it, but they like the salt even more." The vendor told me to come back for more; he'd be available until 9 p.m.

I gave the calves all ten bags of popcorn. Just as they had finished the last bit, the auction officials came around to remove all feed tubs. After that, there would be a per-pound penalty if we fed any more to our calves. The hay that had been available to the calves was taken away in wagons. The calves just looked strange with no feed tubs, no hay, just a little bit of bedding. I kissed them all goodnight. When I stopped to look around, all the other 4-H members from our club were gone. I guess they forgot me.

I walked to the street. I saw buses going by, but I wasn't sure where they were going. I was also confused about routes and changing busses, if that's what I needed to do. I was somewhat familiar with Sioux City, but not by street names. So, I caught a cab to the hotel. That was easy enough.

I had been so busy caring for the calves, then finding my way back to the hotel, I hadn't realized I was hungry. I stopped at the hotel restaurant. There I found a familiar person, the waitress who always waited on my parents and me. She asked me where my folks were. I said something had come up and they had to leave. She asked, "Will you be all right here?"

I said, "Sure, why not?"

"Oh, nothing," she replied.

I ordered my supper.

When I finished my meal, I went straight to my room. On my way, both the bellman and the desk clerk told me that my dad gave them instructions to look after me. Should I need anything, just let them know. They asked if I planned to go out for a movie or something. I said, "No, I need to talk to my dad, then hit the hay." I asked, could they please call me at 5 o'clock as I need to be out in front of the hotel to catch my ride at 5:45.

I went to my room, locked the door, then secured the chain, just as Mom and Dad taught me. I crawled in bed. Then I picked up the phone to call home, collect.

Dad asked me if I was okay. I said. "Yes, but I need to check to see if I've done something I shouldn't have."

I could hear concern in Dad's voice. He asked, "What did you do?"

I told him about the popcorn. He started laughing. Well, that was a good sign. Dad laughed until he started coughing.

He settled down enough to ask some questions. "How much? How were they acting when you left them? How were their eyes, their ears, their breathing? Did they appeared stressed in any way?"

Dad asked what had possessed me to feed the calves popcorn. I told him that I was eating the popcorn myself, I bought it for me not the calves. When the calves came over to me, it was obvious they really wanted some. I also told him what I thought about the salt.

"Sweetheart, you've come up with a very good idea. If it works you're calves will gain weight instead of losing the three-percent that buyers are counting on.

"Are you tired?" he asked.

I told him, "A little."

Dad reminded me that I had a big day tomorrow. "The Paulsons are going to pick you up in the morning at six. Make sure you pack all of our things. I've already paid for the room, so you wait for the Paulsons outside, in front of the door. Don't have them waiting on you. You get down there and wait for them. If you need help, call the bellman. You know what you have to do with your calves, right?"

I said, "Yes. I take them for water. Then I groom them as if I were going in the show ring."

Dad said, "You're a smart girl. Be careful. Your calves weight nearly twelve-hundred pounds. I'm figuring they'll be very thirsty from the popcorn and salt. They'll want their water. You may have trouble with them pulling you off your feet to get a drink; and you may have a problem getting them away from the water, but that's okay. Just let your calves drink. You've lived with them for six months. You should be okay. If you loose control, there will be a herdsman there. He works for the show. He may want to help, but you do your best to not need help.

"I'm so proud of you, honey. You've come up with a very bright idea. Are you worried about being there alone?"

I told him, "No, I'm just tired."

Dad told me to call the desk for a wake-up call right when we hang up.

I said, "I already told them, but I'll double check."

Dad said, "That's my girl." Then he added, "Is the door locked and the chain on?" He reminded me that should anyone knock, do not answer or unlock the door. Get on the phone. Call the desk to tell them what's going on. Don't answer, just call downstairs.

Then Dad asked, "Do you have any questions?"

I said, "No"

Dad said, "Here's your mother."

I spoke with Mom for a few minutes. She reminded me to be clean and presentable. She particularly wanted me to comb my hair so I would look as good as I have the calves looking. I always did a great job grooming the calves. I won Showmanship a number of times at other shows. Mom wanted me to look good in the auction ring. Maybe the calves would bring more income if everything about them was just right. She also told me she was proud of me. She affirmed what a big girl I was. I was tired. I think she could hear it in my voice, so she said, "Good night."

Here I am, a bit shy of 10 years old, staying in a hotel by myself, in a city far from home. Yet, I had such trust in my folks, and they in me, that I knew they wouldn't ask me to do anything that would put me in a bad situation. They could trust me to be responsible for myself as well as my critters. Dad shored up the situation by having the hotel people watch out for me, too. Under similar circumstances, today, parents should fear being thrown in jail for child abuse or abandonment. My, how times have changed.

The next day, everything went according to plan.

Dad was right. A twelve-hundred-pound calf can go anywhere it desires when restrained only by an eighty-pound girl. Yet, they weren't too much out of control.

As expected, they were really thirsty. They didn't want to leave the water, either. They gained weight. I think they were the only calves at the auction that did.

A few weeks later at the traditional 4-H banquet, the speech I gave went well thanks to Mom's guidance.

So you see, just because someone is in the spotlight, or receiving accolades, it doesn't mean they are alone in their achievement. A championship performance is often backed by personnel—I call them partners—supplying guidance, coaching, training, financial and emotional support, safety, security, etc.

Putting things in perspective, when my calves were sold I was able to put $5,000 in my personal bank account. That was 1945 when Median Income was $2379 per family per the Census Bureau. That was a lot of money! Today, Median Income is nearly $50,000; a champion calf could sell for $100,000 to $225,000 or more. That, too, is a lot of money.

Notes:

Jay Durnil:

My son, Jay Durnil, was a remarkable kid, but at first I thought he was like every other kid, that is until he was about three. I looked around at other children and noticed the relationships they had with their mothers.

In what appears to be my family tradition, I raised Jay to be strong, independent, to stand on his own two feet, and speak with good manners. Jay was much more than a child; soon he was my best friend, my defender, and my partner.

Jay with his dogs in 1973. This picture from an article in Omaha's Sunday World Herald.

I decided early that I was not going to be always saying, "No," to Jay as I had heard so many women in grocery and department stores saying, "No," to their children. Not surprisingly the children would pick up on the communication and say, "No, no, no," back to the mothers. So I decided, that when needed, I would just say, "Don't," at a firm tone level.

Jay seemed to have a great affinity with other children and animals. When he was at the crawling age of his life, I heard Jim, the leopard dog,[26] who wouldn't let Jay touch him but was always within three feet of him, start whining with an unusual

---

[26] The Catahoula Cur or Louisiana Catahoula Leopard Dog, is named after Catahoula Parish in the state of Louisiana in the United States. Of remaining dog breeds, the Catahoula is believed to have occupied North America the longest, aside from the dogs descended from Native American-created breeds. (Wikipedia)

sound. I went to the hallway. There I found Jay playing with this new, fun toy. It was a scorpion. He would touch the head, then it would swing around to sting with its tail. Jay would touch the head again and the scorpion would just swing around again. Jim knew it was dangerous. I just told Jay, "Don't." I picked him up, then took him to another place with a different toy.

By the time Jay was two, we had two other dogs, but it was Jim who was always there to protect. We were living in Cushing, Oklahoma. Jerry, Jay's dad, had acquired about fifteen horses. He was keeping them in a local pasture about a mile and a half from the house. Jerry was often out on the road with his sales work; it was my job to feed the horses if he was gone. Early one morning, Jay, the dog Jim, and I went to feed the horses. Jay and Jim were playing fetch with a stick, outside the pasture in a large, clearing area. I was scattering hay and pellets for the horses. I heard Jim yelp. I turned around to see what was going on. Jim was on the outside of the fence, Jay was inside walking among the mares, colts, and a couple of studs.

I gave a hand signal indicating Jim should "Stay." Jay was busy talking to the horses. He was walking under their bellies and hugging their front legs. He was talking to and touching every one of them. I held my breath. I encouraged Jay to follow me or come to me over the shortest distance from the horses. I said, "Let's go," yet Jay went on with what he was doing. I jumped in the car, then started it. Still he wasn't coming. I turned the car around. No response from Jay. Finally I called, "Jay I need you to help me with this feed for the horses. Come help me, okay?" Jay said, "Okay," then walked out to me. That brought just a second of relief. Jay came to me from the backside of the colts, under a couple of saddle horses.

I stood very, very still and waited. My heart was pounding. When he arrived by the feed, I hugged him and asked him to never do that again. He said, "Mom, they wouldn't hurt me. I can talk to them. They just know I love them." I told him that I understood, but I didn't really understand. I told him after this, if he came with me, he would have to promise to stay by my side. He would have his own feed bucket, but he couldn't wander like that again. Jay said, "Okay," and he kept his word.

My marriage to Jerry slowly dissolved. He started drinking to excess. When he lost his job he started hanging out with other women. That left Jay and me with no food in the house. In June, before Jay was three, Jerry took us back to my dad's place. When we arrived, even though Dad knew we were coming, the house was not ready for us to move in. It was really dusty. There was no hot water on tap. Jerry went to town and there he found a 25-gallon, used, hot-water heater belonging to a friend of Dad's.

The friend and Jerry installed the heater. They drank beer all the while. After they had the heater installed, my dad's friend left. Jerry went downstairs to the basement to flip the metal switch "on" while standing in about two inches of water. I tried to stop him and he started getting physical with me. He knocked me down, then jumped on top. Jay wiggled in between us, hitting Jerry. Jay started crying, "Don't you hurt my mama. Don't you hurt my mama." Jerry backed off, went up stairs to fetch another beer, then turned on the TV. In about twenty minutes the water was hot so Jerry drove away. We didn't hear from him again until Christmas.

I found a job working at an advertising agency in Omaha. I had to place our furniture in storage, yet I managed to have two of Jerry's colts sent to us at the farm. With their good bloodlines they might be good-running quarter horses and, as such, they were a good investment. One was named Dancer, the other one was called Nothin'.

One Sunday I was working in the feedlot fixing fence. Jay was with me. He had some ears of corn in his feed-bucket. Dancer came from behind and reached over Jay's shoulder to nibble the corn that Jay was shelling. Jay put his arms around Dancer's neck, close to the back of his head. Jay told him, "Dancer, I just

love you." Again my heart was in my throat. Dancer just kept on eating. Nothin' joined them. The two were gobbling up each kernel as Jay hand-shelled it.

At first, I had no one to care for Jay while I was tending to my day job. I asked an aunt for help. My aunt had several grandchildren but none were like Jay. She said he would talk to the hogs. He would go to the corncrib to obtain armfuls of ear corn. He would shell the corn until his bucket was as full as he could carry. Then, Jay would take it to the hogs to feed them. My aunt said, "He does that all day, every day." She said, "He tells me, 'That's my job.'"

Jay and I went to Kansas City for Christmas. His grandparents and the whole family made Christmas the most joyous occasion ever. Jay had so much fun playing with his cousins. Jay's "Gran-Gran" and I were wrestling, just playing around with a dishtowel while washing dishes. He grabbed me in play. Jay came running towards us, climbed on a chair, jumped on his granddad's back, kicking and screaming, "Don't you hurt my mama. Don't you hurt mama." His granddad had to nearly peel Jay off his back. He tried to calm Jay down and assure him that he wasn't going to hurt me, that we were just playing. Then, of course, Jay wanted to be in my arms. I knew what had triggered the outburst, but I didn't tell "Gran-Gran."

The next spring, Dad and I were working on a horse deal with about thirty Shetland ponies when Jay came in to tell us his pony was getting away. We both went outside to see. The pony was just walking along the tall hedge between the house yard and the feedlot. We caught the pony, then Dad threw Jay in the saddle and said, "Jay you ride that pony. Don't you let him buffalo you."

Jay was showing how he could control the pony with neck reining. I turned to flip the BBQ ribs. Behind me I heard Dad say, "Catch me, I'm falling." I tried to catch him, but I think he was dead before he hit the ground. Jay quieted the pony and sat there. The dogs came also.

Here we are skiing in Steamboat Springs, CO. Jay and I went out for two weeks for three years running. We took our food, a Christmas tree decorations, posters, a stereo, and pretended to be rich. Then we went back to taking care of cattle and working.

Two days after the funeral I sat Jay down on the back stoop where most of this happened. I began telling Jay that Grandpa French was in heaven, probably herding cows and having a good time. I wanted Jay to know that he and his pony had nothing to do with Dad's death. Jay said, "Oh, no Mom," as he quickly corrected me with a firm, "Grandpa French is here and I talk to him all the time." For some reason I didn't try to convince Jay otherwise; I just acknowledged him. If Jay was comforted by that thought, then it was okay with me. However, Jay and I shared strange dreams on the same nights, dreams that involved Dad holding identical conversations with each of us.

During the summer Jay and I took off for Disneyland in Los Angeles. On the way, we stopped in Las Vegas. When Jay dressed to go out, he wore a Western-style corduroy jacket, Western-cut pants, boots, and a Western hat. We went to see Glen Campbell at the International Hotel. I tipped the maître d'. In a jiffy, Jay was seated on the edge of the stage. Ann Murray was the opening act.

I think she must have told Mr. Campbell that there was a kid on the stage. He came out to sang his opening number.

When he finished, Mr. Campbell walked over to Jay. He asked Jay if he would be okay with talking to him on the stage. Jay looked at me. I said, "Whatever you want."

Jay said, "Yes, sir."

The conversation on stage went something like this: "What's your name?"

"Jay Durnil."

Glen said, "Well, Jay, you look like a real cowboy."

Jay replied, "Yes sir, I am."

Glen asked, "Really? Do you have a pony?"

Jay replied, "Yes, sir and I have four breed heifers."

Glen exclaimed, "Wow, you have more cattle than I do and I don't have a pony either."

Jay just smiled.

Glen asked, "Do you play the guitar?"

Jay replied, "No, sir, but I plan to get one when I sell my calves."

Glen said, "You certainly are polite."

Jay responded, "That's the way my mother wants me to talk."

Glen finished the exchange, "Jay when you get that guitar, you can play it with a pick just like mine."

Glen gave him a pick, then escorted Jay back to where we were sitting.

One evening while at Disneyland, we decided to eat at a restaurant outside the hotel. Jay ordered a steak. When the waiter returned with the steak, he asked Jay if he wanted catsup or steak sauce. Jay told him that a good steak did not require catsup or steak sauce. Jay tried to cut his steak. He took a bite, then he waived the waiter to come back over. Jay said, "This *needs* steak sauce." The waiter brought him his steak sauce.

Jay had been dining out with me since he was four. During our time together, I taught him how to be gentlemanly in asking a woman if she cared for a cocktail, inquire what she would like to eat, report to the waiter, and figure a tip.

About the time Jay was turning just over five years, I had my life plan in progress. We were sitting at the dinning room table when Jay announced that he was working on his own plan. I asked him what it was. He said, "I'm going to be the greatest race horse veterinarian in the world." I asked, "Where do you plan to go to school?" He said his dad went to Kansas State. Did they have a vet school? I said, "Yes, one of the best in the country." I quickly added that if he wanted to go there, he would have to pay for the first four years; I would pay for vet school. On his graduation, I would set him up in practice.

Jay's vision was to study hard with the expectation of graduating from high school when he was sixteen. He thought he wasn't smart enough to earn an academic scholarship, so he asked, did K-State have a wrestling team? I told him, "Yes." He said that his dad's cousin has a wrestling scholarship there. The cousin told Jay that he would teach him. First he had to start lifting weights. He didn't have any weights, so Jay was going to do his workouts lifting feed sacks. I had the feed store load thirty-five-pound bags as I thought fifty-pound bags would be too heavy for him.

When he was six, Jay wanted to help with the chores. I attached blocks of wood to the clutch and brake pedals of an old pickup. Jay could reach the throttle for gas. In the mornings I fed the cattle at headquarters. Then, I loaded the truck so Jay could feed them in the evenings, after school. Later on, we had a similar routine with the tractor. Jay delivered silage with the bucket on front.

Jay knew how to acquire and use his resources. We had a stream going through our pasture. I had to stop Jay from driving the tractor when he decided to make a dam so he could stock it with fish for his own fishing hole.

That summer, Jay's twelve year-old cousin from a ranch in Kansas came to visit. She was with us for a week or so. I was having one-hundred-ten calves delivered from Florida. They came in a single truckload. The calves were unloaded into the catch pen. A squeeze-chute was already set up. I was finishing up with canning beet pickles when the two ran into the house. As proud as could be, Jay announced that he had sorted all the calves, sick for well, and they had given the sick ones a shot. "Do you want us to castrate them?"

I couldn't believe what I was hearing. First, I asked Jay how much medication he gave them? He showed me. That was right. I wondered how he knew exactly what to do. Could he have been paying attention when I was treating a sick calf? I went outside with the kids.

I asked Jay on the way out, did you keep them separated? He said, "Yes." I looked at the ones he had given a shot. There was no mistake. I looked at the ones he didn't give a shot. He didn't make a mistake there either.

Later on as his plan started to progress, Jay talked to our vet. He told the doctor of his plans. Then Jay asked if he could have a job when he was fourteen, working the next three summers. Jay further added that all he wanted in pay was a letter of recommendation to vet school. Our vet agreed.

Jay and I on our way to the Cadillac Ball. This was a charity event to raise money for the Pratt School. Jay was the only student to attend the event.

Next, Jay talked to a family friend who was a state senator. The senator owned the sale-barn where we sold our calves. He told Jay he would write him a letter of recommendation. Jay continued his workouts lifting sacks of grain. He attended weekend wrestling matches even though the school didn't have a team there. Later on, he would enter matches. Jay often won the first round on strength alone, but he had a lot to learn when it came to moves and holds. When Jay found out about a wrestling clinic held by a coach from the University of Nebraska at Omaha every summer, Jay insisted that I sign him up even though it was for high school boys. Jay went to the summer camp for as many weeks as they held it. The older boys worked with him. The coach told me that he had never been around a kid, especially that young, who had such drive to meet his goal.

When Jay was eight I set him up with his own checking account. I taught him about finance. He helped when it came time to pay bills. As I worked with him, Jay developed an understanding of what it cost to run a household, what it cost to raise an acre of corn, an acre of beans, and a calf. He knew about interest rates, the stock market, gold, silver, corn, and beans. He accompanied me to the bank when I borrowed money, and again when I paid off the loan. In practical matters, Jay was a willing, attentive student.

We had an airplane in those days. I taught Jay how to land it in case there was ever a problem with the pilot.

Just before the Thanksgiving holiday, we went to the American Royal Horse Show on its final night. We were settled in our seats when Jay went to buy something. It turned out to be a T-shirt from a shop in the vender area. When Jay came back to show me what he had bought, I asked him how he had paid for it.

Jay said, "I gave the man a check."

I said, "Lets go see the man."

Jay asked, "Did I do something wrong?"

I said, "No, it's just that I want to assure the man that your check is okay."

When we arrived at the booth I asked the vendor if he had sold Jay the T-shirt. He said, "Yes." I let him know that Jay's check was good. I wondered what Jay gave him for identification? The man said Jay provided him with ID. That would be the ID card that came with the billfold, the one that Jay himself had filled in! I said, "Really?" The vendor said, "Well, he had personalized checks." With that, he seemed to think that Jay and his check were good enough.

One February day in 1974, at 4:30 in the morning the temperature outside was twenty degrees below zero. I climbed to the top of a two-story stack of hay covered with ice. Pulling the first bale of hay from the top, I took a back gainer when the wire broke. As I fell, I reached out catching a tarp. It ripped, but changed my fall enough so that I hit a wooden fence with the right side of my back. Fortunately, I fell into the hay area, not out with the cattle where they could have trampled me to death.

The doctors initially said I was just bruised, but six weeks later when I returned from a business trip in Chicago with one leg not working, the doctors found my back was broken. They wanted to do surgery, but I was certain there was a better way. Almost magically, someone told me about Dr. DeJarnett. I went to see him.

Dr. DeJarnett was a chiropractor in Nebraska City. He had just returned from Japan where he was teaching. He wasn't a bone cruncher, he was a different kind of chiropractor. He put me in a brace to stretch my spine and give me support. He also put me on wedges, that is to say, pieces of material about eight inches long, one under one leg, another under a hip. In about five minutes of this therapy my muscles relaxed, my spine returned to normal. I had only three visits. Between visits Dr. DeJarnett educated me on how to stand and sit to keep my spine properly aligned.

While I was healing, I came up with a plan. I had to bring Jay into it as at this point he was doing all the chores. I was his driver between two places that stood fifteen miles apart, one in Modale, Iowa, the other south of Blair, Nebraska.

In April, WOWT started talks with me aimed at my working there as the first woman to sell TV time. The benefits were considerable: medical care, life insurance, an expense account, scholarships, access to a credit union. None of these perks were offered at the company where I was working.

Working at WOWT was like going on vacation. It seems like only a second, but it was a week or two after I arrived, they sent me to the American Women in Radio and TV Annual Conference in New York City. I had just been elected president of the local chapter. There in New York I met the president of Meredith, a broadcast and publishing company. He talked to me about working up through the company and moving station to station. I thought that sounded great.

Meanwhile at home, Jay was doing all the chores. We talked seriously about getting out of the cattle business until, perhaps, he was older and I was healthier. Jay agreed, but didn't want to sell off the breed cattle. We sold the cattle in Nebraska, then gave up the property lease. We had enough automatic watering devices and feeders to handle the breed cattle, thus eliminating the work and travel associated with early and late feedings.

At the start of the next school year, Jay was having trouble in the Modale School. The teacher told me that Jay was utterly charming. He knew many practical things, including data well above her head. There were times when she had no idea what he was talking about. His teacher told me that Jay could tell her how much it cost to raise an acre of corn or beans. He knew how much it cost to raise a calf, what the stock and commodities markets were doing. When his teacher had to leave the room, she could leave Jay in charge. He would keep order. He used these opportunities to relate one of the many adventures that he and I had on weekends, holidays, and summers. However, when she had to work with other students, he would take advantage and become naughty.

If his teacher asked him to spell a word, Jay would brush the teacher off by telling her that his secretary will spell for him. When doing math, he asked for a calculator. It seems he was already assuming an executive roll. Jay was not reading well aloud, but he could tell his teacher about *Call of the Wild* and *Jonathan Livingston Seagull*, his favorite books. Jay would read and comprehend, just not aloud. He liked to read silently. It was about that time that Jay and I decided he needed to go to another school, maybe a private one in Omaha.

Being good, responsible partners, Jay and I sat down to discuss the problem in the Modale School. I mentioned this private school I knew about not too far from the TV station. Our advantage in making the change would be that we could travel and have more time together. Jay had to agree to apply himself because tuition at this place was costly. He said if he liked it, he would do the school work required. I told him I would keep him company while he cared for our animals, if that's what he wanted.

Private School:

Jay and I interviewed with the school, and they with us. It seems there were many well-known families that had children going there. The school asked us to come back after Thanksgiving Day. They would give us the results of the tests then. They quoted us the fee. That was going to be a challenge.

I called Jerry, Jay's dad. I told him the situation. I thought we should split the cost of school. Jerry agreed. Now, we just had the final challenge of Jay being accepted.

Meanwhile, we went to Steamboat Springs to ski with my friend, Sharon, her boyfriend, Howie, and her two girls, one a year older and one a year younger than Jay. We drove all night to reach our destination, then we drove all night Sunday on the return trip, but we had so much fun.

Jay and I met with representatives of the school late Monday. They told us that the test results indicated that Jay had not learned anything in school since the fourth grade. They said Jay would have to go back and complete, to their standard, six weeks of the third grade, the entire fourth grade, and then complete the fifth grade by the end of school. They told Jay these are the school's standards. He would have to accept them as his own. Did he think he was up to the task? Jay said, "Yes."

Jay and I excused ourselves to review our meeting with the representatives of the school and to firm up our agreements. We spoke for about ten minutes. Jay had a question so Mrs. Pratt joined us. She owned the school. She was ninety-two years old. Jay was concerned about being teased since he would be doing third-grade work. Mrs. Pratt informed us that the school had three classrooms and no one student knew what grade the others were in as it was all private study. The students were aware only of the separation of grade school and high school. She also informed me that every student recited in front of her each day. In addition, the students have to learn manners, know how to serve tea, how to greet and shake hands with an adult. Students were expected to rise when an adult came into the room. Jay was familiar most of that except for the serving of tea.

I said I thought reciting might be a little old-fashioned. Maybe the kids wouldn't do well because they did not enjoy it. Mrs. Pratt informed me that she always had homemade fudge in the bottom drawer of her desk. All seemed to do a good job for the reward. Then she smiled.

Jay and I talked a little more, established our agreement, then I paid the tuition. Jay started the next day.

Two weeks later, Jay informed me that he hated the school and wished he'd never made the agreement. I asked him what was going on. He told me that he practiced penmanship for two hours a day. Then he said, "I have to read out loud for two hours and I have to do math in ink for two hours. The only good thing is I have only six to eight words in spelling." When I called the school they informed me that Jay had a habit of skipping words, so by having him read aloud they could pick it up and correct him. Writing in ink helped him to think before he put down an answer as he would guess, then just keep writing different answers.

In six weeks Jay was happy, his writing was beautiful, his math was so much better, his reading was great. He told me that the assigned words in spelling were important because every word had the same spelling rule. By sounding out the words, he had learned how to spell. He now liked the school.

Private Lakes:

Our interests were getting further and further away from Modale.
I asked Jay if he would be happy in Omaha. He said it would have
to be a place where he didn't think it was the city. So we started
looking for a place to call home in Omaha. First, we looked at
houses with swimming pools in West Omaha. Then we went on
out about 25 miles to a place where all the houses had 5 to 10
acres and a barn. He liked that area a lot. Then we went another
5 miles out to Private Lakes where there were stocked lakes, a
barn for horses, and maybe his prize-bred heifer. To add to the
country feel, there were farms all around the lakes. Across the
road toward the little town there was a horse farm. Jay thought
that would be the best place. He would be happy there.

We put our farming headquarters in Modale up for sale. Then
I wrote a contract to have a new place built on the main lake at
Private Lakes. The new owners of our place in Modale were going
to tear down all the buildings, so Jay and I went ahead tearing down
the old corncrib. We could use that weathered wood in Jay's new
bedroom. It would make it look like a bunkhouse. The old front
door had etched glass with a stag and wolves. It was going to be
placed into the doorway coming from the garage. The etched glass
from the old bay window went into my headboard in my bedroom.
I tried to bring with me as much as I could from the old place.

It took longer to finish the house at Private Lakes than planned.
We moved into a small efficiency apartment within walking
distance of Jay's school and the TV station. We were there for
two months and then moved into our new place in February.

Jay wanted a special bedroom to bring his friends. I thought that
was a good idea. When it was finished, Jay's room was incredible.
He had a queen-size bunk bed. Restored and electrified kerosene
lamps from our old barn hung from the beams. There was a

Hereford hide on one wall with an oil painting of two Hereford bulls fighting. Two wranglers were roping them around the horns to pull them apart. Below that Jay had his antique, hexagon-barrel .22 rifle. His saddle rested on a saddle rack on the opposite wall where a long desk, book shelves, cabinets and drawers were located. The furniture was stained to match the barn siding. Jay's fishing poles and skis were also mounted on the wall.

Fence posts extended from the floor to the ceiling to hold the bunk beds in place. On one of the posts he put a name tag and hung a cow skull. The indoor-outdoor carpet was an American Indian pattern. We used indoor-outdoor carpet because it would be easier to clean. No doubt there would be spills when cleaning guns, polishing leather, etc.

Jay's bath was chocolate embossed leather from Spain. The bathroom cabinet was painted to look like leather. The ceiling was covered in copper tile. The walls and floor were chocolate tile. The bath was well lighted. The entire room was covered in western decorations.

One of Jay's favorite things was his train set that was permanently mounted on plywood. He could turn the set on edge and store it in his walk-in closet.

Spring:

April in Nebraska is usually pleasant and warm. Winter was behind us and Jay's creative juices were flowing with a couple of business ideas. He put out flyers advertising a service for dog and plant sitting, available in the evenings and on weekends. Time to deliver the service was limited by Jay's schedule at school. He also had his new fourteen-foot sailboat tied at our dock. It's likely this new possession prompted Jay's next idea: He tried to persuade me to let him operate a fuel station for boaters in the area. Our truck had a 150-gallon tank with a pump in the back. The boat dock was right by our house. At first Jay wanted a 100 percent markup on gasoline, but later agreed that 20 percent would be fair. After all, these customers would also be our neighbors and I felt it was a good idea to maintain friendly relations.

We decided to have a housewarming party on Saturday, May 1, 1976. I invited two-hundred people from my community. Jay invited thirty-seven of his friends from Modale, Omaha, and kids from his school.

It was April 29. I was sitting in the kitchen working on lists for a scavenger hunt for the kids and adults. The food and drinks were laid in. Jay had gone to his tree house. It was down by the Elkhorn River that ran on the east side of the development, about a half-mile from the house.

I was working on my lists when, suddenly, Jay came running up from the lakeside, through the house, and up the stairs to his room. He came back down, two steps at a time, then ran out the door. Before he disappeared, I said, "Hey, Jay, wait a minute! Where are you going? It is almost dark!"

Jay said his new friend had a pellet gun. They were going to shoot cans down at the river. We lived in a gated community so I assumed the new friend was another kid. I said, "Okay, but be back here twenty minutes before dark. Okay?" He said, "Okay," turned to jump on his bike, then he rushed back to me. He gave a kiss, a big hug, and said, "Catch you on the flip-flop.[27] We gone. Bye-bye."

Twenty minutes passed: I began to worry, just a little as any mother would. I walked outside, looked down the road to the river, no sign of Jay. I backed the car out of the garage, then started a more intensive search. I went over to Jay's tree house, driving as close as the road would allow. I stepped out of the car, walked to the edge of the road, and yelled. I had a yell that

---

[27] CB radio slang, flip-flop = return trip

Jay knew was especially for him. I used it when we were out in the country. That yell would rattle windows. Yet, no answer: I stepped back into the car, then drove slowly around all the roads leading to both lakes. The sky was still a bit light. I continued looking for Jay or his bike thinking it might be in someone's yard, like maybe the boys had gone to another boy's home.

I returned to the house and walked through. Jay's favorite trick was to hide, then he would jump out to scare me. He often succeeded. This time I would be more relieved than scared, but nothing:

Just then, the phone rang. I thought it must be Jay calling. It wasn't: The call was from a friend who lived a couple of doors from us. Mr. Hatch was calling to visit, as neighbors do. When Frank asked what I was up to, I said, "Looking for Jay."

I learned that Frank was busy putting up a fence when Jay rode by on his bicycle. He wanted to ask Jay for help, but Jay was quickly gone towards the river, down on the old road, past the barn and corrals. Tex, the dog, was running beside him. I believe my neighbor was the last one to see Jay that day.

We went out in Frank's car. Combing the neighborhood, we spoke with everyone we could find who happened to be out in their yard. No one had seen Jay:

When Frank and I arrived back at the house, Tex was there. We went inside searching the house again. Still no sign of Jay: Now I am really concerned and thinking I should call the law. The Sheriff's Deputies arrived about 10:30 that night. They took a description of Jay and wrapped up our meeting saying they would bring dogs out for a search in the daylight. In the morning, I took them down to Jay's tree house, but they saw nothing out of the ordinary leaving us with no clue.

Outwardly, I was being brave, yet I was troubled inside. I needed support so I turned to Sue Hollins, my personal coach. She and her boyfriend, Donnie, came out to my place the following night. Sue and Donnie arrived about 11:30 p.m. It was over 24 hours since Jay had come up missing. Sue was able to give me the support I needed. Once my nerves were calmed, we decided to walk instead of driving around the streets of the neighborhood. Donnie brought a flash light. He went down to examine Jay's tree house while Sue and I waited on the road. Nothing: We continued to search until almost 1:30 in the morning. Sue had to go to work in a few hours, so we all went to bed. I slept fitfully.

Tex was acting peculiarly. He would approach Jay's bedroom, but not go in. Tex would go up to the doorway, lie down, then whine. If he wasn't whining by Jay's bedroom door, he would be in my bedroom close to my side of the bed. About 4:00 in morning a ball of light moved into the bedroom. It paused briefly at the foot of the bed; then it moved out: Tex stood up, whimpered, then he laid back down.

It was now Friday morning. I called my office to say I would not be coming in. Outside, a helicopter was flying over the lakes and woods; guys in boats were busy dragging the river.

Inside the house, Tex and I were all alone. We sat for a spell on the living room floor. Had he been able to talk, I am certain he would have told me what I most needed to know. "Tex, where's Jay?" Unfortunately, Tex could not say. So, there I sat hugging a one-hundred-twenty-pound dog wondering what the heck was going on. That was the first and only time I cried. I realized I was feeling sorry for myself, the important thing was Jay and his whereabouts.

I needed to make phone calls, first to my banker, then my accountant. I wanted to raise as much money as I could in case of a demand for ransom.

By late afternoon, I had put together about $225,000 in cash. Then people started showing up. Among those who showed up was a detective assigned to the case, Jim Whittle, and a couple of my friends. I called Jerry, Jay's dad, to see if by some strange reason Jay had taken a plane to Jerry's place. Jerry made a heated remark that I'm sure he regretted. I hung up the phone. I was directing my energies at finding Jay. I was not going to defend myself to anyone at this point.

The question of Jay's whereabouts was on the noonday broadcast from the TV station. Ann Peterson, a good friend of mine and the first anchorwoman at the station, nearly lost her composure when the news hit. She, Jay, and I had been driving golf balls just the previous Saturday. Everyone at the station knew Jay because he usually walked there every day from school.

My friend, Pat Nolan, showed up at the house Friday about noon. She called all the people who Jay and I had invited to the party. Another friend, Bobbie Powell, slept on a chair with her hand on the phone all night, so if anyone called I would not be disturbed. I was exhausted. I had stopped talking on the phone at noon.

Law enforcement officials would not do a missing-persons report for seventy-two hours, so the weekend was spent with many people coming and going while I was stuck in a waiting game.

My coach, Sue, committed to living with me during this distressing time. She insisted that if in the middle of the night I needed help or someone to talk to, I should wake her. Having someone to talk to, someone skilled at listening, was very important to me. More than talk, however, we worked together for about an hour each night reviewing and evaluating all the emotions, physical sensations, pains and other feelings that I was having regarding Jay and his mysterious absence. Those hours spent in consultation each night kept me cool, calm, and thinking clearly during the day.

Saturday, I started a search for a private investigator. I was specifically looking for one known for finding stolen or otherwise missing children. I needed the investigator who was able to solve every murder case in Douglas County over the past few years. One of the news guys from the station found that private detective for me. I called right away to arrange a meeting.

Denny Whelan and I met on Saturday afternoon. He told me the Sheriff's Office would be displeased if I hired him, but he said, "I also have people who will talk to me but not them." Denny used unorthodox methods that reminded me of an entertaining detective one might see on a TV show. To his credit, he had solved every murder case in the county covering the previous five years. He also found and returned three kidnapped children. His performance record was as good as it gets. We made an agreement, Denny was on the payroll.

Saturday night, around 10:00, I had really bad feelings. My coach, Sue, and I walked outside in the cool air. I couldn't put my finger on any particular reason why, but I was nervous, jumpy, cold. I just couldn't figure it out. Later on Monday, I figured out what I was feeling.

Sunday morning Detective Jim came to the house. I told him I had a weird feeling Saturday night. I said, "Let's you and I go to the river." I brought Tex along. When we were both out of the car, I said, "Tex, where's Jay?" Tex ran off taking us down to the river just a few feet from Jay's tree house. There, in the sandy soil, we found clearly visible tire tracks. We also found fresh beer cans and an empty cigarette package. Some targets that Jay used with his pellet gun were lying around. I asked Detective Jim if he wasn't going to have a mold taken of the tracks. I also asked, shouldn't he or his people collect the cans and cigarette butts? There might be someone else's prints on these things. Also, there might be finger prints on Jay's targets, someone besides Jay.

Detective Jim's reply was, "Wanda, we think that you're boy just ran away. He'll call or come back."

I said, "Jim, you went through Jay's room. He keeps bills under 'money' and under 'green' in his encyclopedia. He also keeps loose change under his mattress. If he's going to run away, he would at least cop one of my credit cards and leave when I drop him off at school. He has been traveling since he was four. He knows how to travel. If he runs away, he would not go without his dog. I'm glad I hired Denny Whelan. He's at least looking."

Well, that was the wrong thing to say: I took off in my car, Detective Jim took off in his.

Later that Sunday, the house was filled with many concerned people, there to help in whatever way they could. I served the food that I had laid in earlier for the party. A Lieutenant Demsey and Detective Jim came to see me. We went to my bedroom to speak as there was no place else to go for some quiet. The detectives were not happy with my hiring Denny Whelan. They said it looked bad for me. (My hiring Denny made it look bad for *them*.) I told the detectives I would make a deal with the Devil himself to have my boy back, alive and well. I was going pursue every avenue I could.

There was nothing more I could do at home. When I am upset I return to familiar territory, work. So, on Monday, I went to WOWT. There I started planning "The Great Search." I would pull all my resources together on the coming weekend.

The Great Search:

My plan was to have four teams, three people to a team, two on horseback, one in a truck or car on the nearest road. I would have two teams going north on each side of the river and two teams going south on each side of the river. Each team would be connected by walkie-talkie. They were to check every cabin, trailer, and fishing shack. If an enclosure was locked, the teams were to search as best they could through the windows. Before moving on, they would record the address so the Sheriff could look further into the location.

When I arrived home after work on Monday, Detective Jim was waiting for me. I had to ride with him to the river. As we left the house I could see a swarm of law enforcement cars and remote trucks from all the TV stations in the area. Oh, I feared the worst.

When we arrived at the river, I jumped out of the car, then ran down to where everyone stood. Detective Jim caught up with me. He said a bike was sticking up out of the water. Someone had reported it.

"Was that Jay's bike?" Detective Jim asked.

I said, "Yes." (I think, when I was having all those anxious and weird feelings on Saturday night, that someone was bringing the bike back. The Sheriff's Department had drug the river in that exact spot on the previous Friday with no results.)

I looked around, then asked, "Is there someone here to whom I can tell that this is, officially, Jay's bike?"

A Captain walked up to me. I told him this was Jay's bike. I asked if they were going to expand the search from this location, pulling in what they were doing now. I challenged, why didn't they bring out the dogs last Friday as they said they were going to do? "What is your plan!" Well, the TV cameras were running. I was aggressive. The Captain just kind of stood there. It did not look good for the authorities; I was not the collapsing mother.

Between hiring Denny and that confrontation in front of the cameras, the people at the Sheriff's Office were not happy with me. The following Friday, I received my first lie detector test. From that point, they started interrogating me almost nightly. Then the *Sun*, a national, yellow journalism newspaper,[28] called the Sheriff's Office. The reporters from the paper also called *me*. The story hit the newsstands the following week. That was another ding on the public image of the Sheriff's Office. So, we had another lie detector test.

Every interview was recorded. They were performing voice stress tests off the recordings. At the time I did not realize everything they were doing with the tests.

The "Great Search" yielded no results:

Jay's dad, Jerry, came to the search accompanied by his best friend. The two were in a bass boat; they went up the river twenty miles and down the river twenty miles, too.

Tuesday, I called a press conference. I offered $25,000 for any information leading to the arrest of whoever took my boy.

Jerry had hooked up with an Indian in Oklahoma who was a recommended psychic. The Sheriff's Office still had questions for me, so we met every night to "go over it one more time." My coach, Sue, was still living with me. We would wrap up each day in consultation for at least an hour a session.

---

[28] Yellow journalism, journalism that downplays legitimate news in favor of eye-catching headlines that sell more newspapers.

Early Thursday morning around 3:00, I woke Sue and said, "It's starting to get to me. We need to talk."

I wasn't crying but I was trying to figure out my responsibility or lack of, what I could have done, so this would not have happened. We took a dictionary from the bookshelf, then looked up the word *responsibility*. We discussed that word forward, backward, sideways, up, and down. I could see no way I was responsible. This was my conclusion: Jay had a dog with him that would kill for him—there was no doubt about that. Jay was simply in the wrong place at the wrong time, trusting the wrong person.

Jerry called me on a Tuesday to tell me that his Indian friend said Jay was on the move north of downtown Omaha. The psychic saw Jay on the edge of the Missouri River or in a small boat headed north. I started at the bridge between Omaha and Council Bluffs from downtown. I stopped at every business, including the Army Corps of Engineers. Then I went on up the road to a fish restaurant which was the last business north of Omaha on the Missouri River. No one had seen anyone, especially Jay.

The next day my secretary called to tell me the Sheriff's Office wanted me to come there "as soon as possible." When I arrived they took me to the Captain's office. They told me they had found a body, but they didn't know if it was Jay. They said I would have to identify it. I said, "No." (I wanted to remember Jay as he was, alive.) I told them they had what they needed in fingerprints and dental records. The officers left me there, alone, in that office for about four hours.

I didn't know it, but while I waited in the office, news was on the radio and TV that the authorities had found a young person's body in the Missouri River. My coach, Sue, along with one of my best friends, Howie, with whom we went skiing on Thanksgiving Day, heard the report. They were sitting outside the office door where I waited, but the officers would not tell me, nor would they let them in to see me.

Finally, the Captain came in. He said they had identified the body as Jay Durnil. I don't know what kind of reaction he expected, but he didn't get it. I turned and looked at the wall for an instant. Then I turned back. I walked fast in front of him, pointed my finger in his face, then I said, "Don't you dare sweep this one under the rug as you have the other three children's deaths in this area. I won't let that happen." I was enraged.

I asked the Captain if he had any reason for me to remain there. He said, "No." I said, "You get all the information from that body you can because when you release it, it will be cremated."

What a surprise when my friends, Sue and Howie, were waiting outside the office door. We all headed to my house. When we arrived, officers were there. They wanted permission to search the house. I said, "Sure."

The three of us went out on the patio taking in a view of the lake. We each had a glass of wine. We discussed what was going on with me, mentally, emotionally. Mostly they listened as I talked and paced a little back and forth. Tex looked like he was crying. The officers came out with a list of items they were going to take. I signed it without much looking it over.

I finally let go: "I guess we'd better plan the funeral."

When the body was released, it would be cremated. We would have a rosary the night before the funeral. I would display Jay's picture and his cowboy hat adorned with a single rose on the brim. At the funeral we would have Richard Harris' rendition of *Jonathan Livingston Seagull*, Jay's favorite book.

Sue, Howie, and I figured the Sheriff's Office must have notified Jerry as when I called his wife, she said Jerry knew. He was already on his way to Omaha. Just about the time the plans were made, I called the funeral home. I had the minister plus a friend who was a deacon to do the rosary. Jerry arrived, barging into my house without knocking or ringing the doorbell. He was drunk. He jumped me for not looking after Jay properly. How dare I arrange the funeral without his approval? I was astonished. Here was a man who paid me no child support, not ever, nor did he make much effort to see his son until his recent marriage.

Sue and Howie stepped in. "Jerry you need to settle down or leave." Jerry called them a few choice names, then he left slamming the door behind him. He peeled out of the drive. He went straight away to the morgue. There he demanded to see Jay. As I said, I never wanted to see Jay in the morgue because of how I wanted to remember him, vibrant and alive.

The Sheriff's Officers were at the funeral taking photographs of everyone who attended. The funeral home had two stories. It was filled with people also standing outside. Some time after the funeral, I went to the Sheriff's Office for a review of all the pictures they had taken.

My older cousin, Ken, was twenty years older than me. He was a farmer in the midst of corn-planting season, but Ken was around for support as much as he could be. When it came time to scatter Jay's ashes, Ken was with Jerry and me. We went to Steamboat Springs to scatter Jay's ashes on his favorite ski slope. When our little ceremony was over, Jerry left for Kansas City from Denver, Ken and I went back to Omaha. We arrived at the house about 9:30 at night. I said to everyone, Kenneth, his wife Gerri, Sue, Donnie, and Howie, "It's time for me to be alone. You've all been so wonderful, but you need to be with your own families. Tex and I need to be alone." Everyone honored my request and left.

I think the last person to leave had just shut the door when the phone rang. It was the Sheriff's Office asking me to come in the next morning. I told them I planned to sleep in. I was tired. It had been a long three weeks. I told them I would be in at 11:00 in the morning.

The vice president of Union Pacific was a friend who had helped me look for Jay from the beginning. He called. I asked him if he was going to his office on Sunday, as usual. He said, "Yes."

I asked, "Can I hitch a ride and you drop me off at the Sheriff's Office?"

He said, "Sure." On the way in, he asked, "I probably won't be back for three hours. Will that be okay?"

I replied, "Sure. I can just wait for you."

Little did I know, the Sheriff's Office had other plans. They had me wait for three hours while they paraded different people in front of me. I told the officers that I knew none of them. Furthermore, I had never even seen any of them before. Then the officers asked if they could give me one more lie detector test. Their justification was the people who had done it before didn't know what they were doing. This test was going to be done by an expert from Chicago. I agreed.

When I sat down in the chair, I knew this man was different. He was all business, stern, no Mr. Nice Guy.

The test questions have to be answerable as "Yes" or "No." There's a certain degree of discomfort because of the chair, the cord around your chest, and the blood-pressure cuff on your arm. The examiner has to release it every so often, but your hand usually goes to sleep anyway. At least, mine did. The administrator of the test is to never come within three feet of the person being tested as his proximity, alone, can influence the results.

After asking some baseline questions, he launched into a different set of questions, brutal, offensive, completely irrelevant as far as I was concerned. This was nothing like going over the story to see if I had forgotten anything.

"Are you a lesbian?
"Is Pat Nolan a good friend? Your lover?
"Am I engaged to the janitor at WOWT?
"Did Jay see you having sex with a man?
"Did you have sex with Jay?
"Did you offer a reward because you knew you would never have to pay it?
"Did you pay someone to kill Jay?
"Was Jay killed for the insurance you had on him?
"Did you pay someone to put Jay in the river?
"Did you kill Jay?
"Did you put him in the river?"

The last thing the examiner did was really not legal, as I understand it now. He left his seat, walked in front of me, put his arms out within a foot of me and said, "Can you imagine that I'm carrying Jay, your son, in my arms?"

I said, "Yes."

The examiner asked, "Is he dead?"

I looked him straight in his eyes, then I quietly said, "No." Out of the corner of my eye, I saw the lines were still going straight on the lie detector, as straight as they had been throughout the questioning. That was my reality. The only thing that was dead was Jay's body. The essence of Jay lives on. There was no emotion on my part, just calm certainty.

I think the biggest problem for the Sheriff's Office was they had never been around someone with my attitude and spiritual awareness.

The interview was over. The examiner unhooked me, Detective Jim was waiting at the door. I went to walk out of the room. When I reached the door, I turned and said to the interviewer, "You are a suppressive person."[29] Detective Jim said, "What do you mean?" I said, "Maybe both of you should look it up in a dictionary."

For the first time, I was upset with their tactics. In Jim's office, I saw what I thought was a box of cartridges for my pistol. I asked him if it was mine. He said, "Yes." I told him that was not on the list of items they took from my house. The release I signed had no ammo on it. Detective Jim pulled the file, looked it over, then he said I was right. I told him I wanted the cartridges. He said, he had to have a form signed by the officer who picked them up; that officer was gone for the day. I could come back Monday on my way home from work. The box of cartridges would be at the front desk.

When I picked them up on Monday, there were only 6 cartridges in the box. Before the Sheriff's Office had taken them, the box was full except for the six cartridges I had in my revolver. The sheriffs all used .38-calibers in their handguns, too. What more abuse could I expect?

I had been at the Sheriff's Office for five hours. They did not bother to tell me that my friend, Frank Hatch, was waiting there. By this time I had lost all confidence in the Sheriff's ability.

---

29 Suppressive person: destructive, anti-social personality; a sociopath

Dixie:

Jimmy O'Neal, one of the DJ's from the radio side of WOW, had come to us from California. He cornered me in the hall a day or so later. Jimmy told me of a psychic who worked with police on murder cases in several cities in the United States. Her name was Dixie Utarian. She taught parapsychology at U.C.L.A. where local detectives, as well as regular students, attended her classes. Jimmy said he had Dixie's telephone number, if I wanted to call. If I wanted to call? Of course I did!

Dixie flew to Omaha two weeks later. Limited by previous commitments, she was at the Sheriff's Office for two of her three days in Omaha. The third day she really worked hard. First she and Tex went to the woods by the river. In the morning, I was working at the station. My private detective, Denny, was with Dixie all day. He taped everything Dixie had to say. He logged everything they picked up at the river and from Jay's room where Dixie slept.

Dixie thought the man was fishing, perhaps camping at the river for about ten days before the kidnapping. Dixie's impression of this man was that he had worked for stables in Oklahoma and Texas, so horses were the topic of conversation. Jay was born in Texas. He was intent on becoming a veterinarian. So they had something in common to talk about.

Dixie said the man had accidentally backed over Jay's bicycle and bent the wheel. Jay was upset. That made sense. I told Jay the next time he wrecked his bike he would have to fix it himself. The man told Jay he would take him home, then explain to me that he had bent the bike; it was none of Jay's doing. The man did not want a dog in his pickup, so Jay sent Tex home on his own. Jay climbed into the pickup while the man put Jay's bike in the back under the shell. When the man climbed into the truck, Jay told him, "You're not going to just fix my bike, you're going to buy me a new one." (Jay would have done that.)

With that, the man angered. He grabbed Jay to shake him. Realizing this man was unstable, Jay jumped out of the truck. By this time it was getting dark and difficult to see. As he hit the ground, Jay turned his ankle and fell. The man soon caught up to Jay, hit him in the stomach, dragged him to the pickup, tied his hands behind his back, then threw him on top of his bike. He covered both Jay and the bike with a quilt.

Dixie had a map of the county. She went on to say the man took Jay to King Lake. She pointed to the spot on the map. King Lake was a small village up river about ten miles. It was a really rough area with trailers, campers, some hoodlums on motorcycles, and one grocery store with a bar. Dixie explained that the guy thought he could secure some money there to hit the road with Jay still in the back of the truck. The man had no intention of killing Jay.

Dixie continued with her impression of the event: Jay managed to jump out of the back of the truck. The man caught him, Jay kicked him between the legs, then took off. Jay's hands were still tied. To make matters worse, Jay couldn't run very fast with a sprained ankle.

The man was extremely angry at Jay's actions. He picked up a piece of wood that, as Dixie described, was like a wooden arm from a rocking chair. When he caught up with Jay he swung as hard as he could hitting Jay in the back of the head. Jay died almost instantly. (Verified by the autopsy report.)

Further, Dixie said he threw Jay back into the pickup. The man went north to Highway 64. He drove east to the Missouri River at the Mormon Bridge. He couldn't put Jay in the river there because of a high chain link fence blocking access. The man followed the road south, stopping just a little bit north of the airport; but people were fishing there, so he could not stop. The man continued to follow a road south, past downtown Omaha, out of the county. Dixie indicated that she saw a bridge to the left but high above her; behind her a tall mound of something, and a pier extending out from shore, above the water. That's where he put Jay's lifeless body into the river.

Following the psychics impressions, we hired a boat and went down river to where the Army Corp of Engineers found Jay's body. At that location, Dixie said she felt nothing. We returned to shore, climbed into my car, followed the road along the river, then went south of the South Omaha Bridge. At that location, we found exactly the scene Dixie had described. When Dixie and I went out on the pier, we found what looked like blood. We cut and carefully removed the apparent bloodstained wood, then put it in a plastic bag. This bag and its contents was sent to the Nebraska Crime Lab. To the best of my knowledge, the Sheriff's Office intercepted the package. I don't know what happened to the sample, but the crime lab never received it.

On Denny's advice, I hired a fine artist to sit with Dixie. The artist sketched the person she saw with Jay. Before Dixie left Omaha, Denny had archived nearly five hours of her comments.

When I took Dixie to the airport the next morning she told me she didn't want to come, that she had given up this kind of work because she went through the same pain as the victim, but I had said something that made her feel compelled to assist. I don't know what I might have said. I felt that Jay had some influence, working from the other side, perhaps to give me some peace, an awareness of just what happened.

Many people tried to help find Jay: The governor of the state sent two detectives from the Highway Patrol. They met with too much chaos at the Sheriff's Office, so they left town after just a day. The Sheriff's Office was fielding so many calls that no record was kept, according to the Highway Patrol officers. The Omaha Police pursued a pedophile who lived a couple of blocks from Jay's school. They conducted a raid, found pictures of young boys, none of Jay. The police sent a report to the Sheriff's Office as the pedophile had moved to King's Lake. The Sheriff never opened the file until I called them on it. They wouldn't call the F.B.I. for assistance even after I had called the Sheriff's Office *and* the F.B.I to request that they come into the investigation. I could go on and on with examples of people trying to help and authorities demonstrating incompetence. With all that help on hand, the case was never solved.

However, the Sheriff's Office remained focused on me, keeping track of my actions, including my social dates, for over a year. Denny Whelan checked out other child-murder cases in other parts of the United States, Atlanta being one such area. One man was captured, then convicted of murdering two young boys in our area. The Sheriff's Office was certain this man had murdered Jay, but Denny spent four hours with the man only to find out the guy had all the wrong answers. Together, Denny, Howie, and I uncovered many "dropped balls." The Sheriff's Office simply didn't do their job of leads follow-up until I brought the findings to their attention.

The Sheriff's Office was so busy questioning me that they looked nowhere else. During the three weeks that Jay's whereabouts was unknown, the Sheriff's Office questioned me for about sixty hours, including three lie-detector tests.

About ten years later a new detective and a TV reporter did an unsolved-mystery followup for TV, but it was the coldest of cases then as now.

Nothing is harder to live with than a tragic mystery, particularly one that involves a loved one. Had I not had the world's best coach and friend in Sue Hollins, who protected me from negative people, and who was there for me through all the rough spots, I don't know what would have happened to me. Even with all that personal support, the assistance of friends, neighbors, officials, and others in the community, this loss was the biggest challenge I've ever faced.

As I have stated before, it is my reality that Jay was in the wrong place at the wrong time, trusting the wrong person. In wrestling, Jay was taught to defend himself. He and I discussed how he should deal with strangers. We even talked about the kick to the groin he should use if he ever found himself in trouble.

I think of Jay often. My god, I loved that kid, not the kid who seemed to nickel-and-dime me to death, but the one who had so much to offer the world. I would have given up everything I owned, my very life, to see him mature, contribute, and prosper. I miss him. I shall always regret losing my son, my very best friend, my student, my teacher, my partner.

No matter the age of your children, my wish for you is that you have such a constructive and rewarding relationship with your children as I had with Jay. Moreover, I wish you long, prosperous lives. No matter their age, the children are your students as well as your teachers. They are our partners in life. They are our future.

Notes:

Nathan Novak:

Ah, there's the Gas Lamp Restaurant, famous for prime-ribs. It looks like I'm early, so, I park and wait for my clients to arrive. It's the first time I've been out to eat late at night since I lost Jay.

Just then, the couple I was waiting for, Sid and Barbara, pulled into the parking lot. We met at the door and walked into the restaurant together. While we were waiting to be seated, Nathan Novak left his table. He approached us, he shook Sid's hand, gave Sid's spouse, Barbara, a kiss on the check, and put his arm around my shoulders. Nathan asked, "How are you doing, kid?"

Wanda Durnil
and Nathan Novak

I said, "Okay. You can't keep a good woman down." Nathan motioned to the waitress to bring drinks to our table when we were seated. Then he went back to his table.

The Novaks were a large, wealthy family. They owned multiple businesses. Each sibling was involved at some level of management. There were twelve automobile dealerships in two states. They owned tires, batteries and accessory stores. There was a motorcycle dealership. Their business enterprise varied with storage properties, banks, an insurance company, a restaurant, numerous real estate holdings including commercial, residential, and farms. They owned a high-rise, upscale apartment house called Twin Towers, a prestigious location with its new-occupant waiting list. The main and lower floors of the Twin Towers were business offices, one of which was the main office for Novak

Enterprises. At one time Novak Enterprises was the largest retail business in the state of Nebraska.

I knew of the Novaks because I had handled a couple of their company advertising accounts when I was at Smith-Kaplan. Nathan could be very demanding when you worked for him. On the other hand, he was very generous in his contributions to the community. Nathan had called early in Jay's disappearance to see if there was anything his family could do to help find him. Then a few weeks later, Nathan offered three of the family limos for Jay's funeral. At the time, I thanked him, but I didn't take advantage of his offer because we had Jay's body cremated.

As we sat down at our table, I said to Sid and Barbara, "What in the world is wrong with Nathan Novak? I've never known him to be so friendly and so dressed down. And, what's with that full beard?"

Barbara said, "Didn't you know, his wife has started divorce proceedings."

I said, "No, I wonder what she did?" I went on, "When I was handling one of his accounts for the agency, I sent his table a round of drinks. At the next ad meeting we had, he told me not to ever do that again. He didn't want any possibility of anyone spreading rumors that would hurt or offend his wife or family."

Nathan came by our table on his way out of the restaurant to say goodbye. He commented on how it was good to see us. He had the waitress bring us after-dinner drinks when we were ready for them. He put the drinks on his tab. (Barb and I were not drinking in those days, but we didn't say, "No." I don't think people said, "No," to Nathan very often, if at all.)

When I worked with Nathan a couple of years earlier, he always dressed as if he had just stepped out of *GQ*.[30] Now, he was wearing casual slacks, an open shirt, and a rough out-jacket. He sported a full, multicolored beard.

About twenty minutes after Nathan left our table, I was paged. Since Jay had been gone only six months, the first thing that flashed in my mind was, "Is Jay okay?" I dismissed the thought replacing it with, "Who knows I'm here?"

When I said, "Hello," the voice on the other end said, "I hope you don't mind that I called you away from your guests."

I said, "No."

The voice asked, "Do you know who this is?"

I said, "Of course, we've talked many times on the phone and I know your voice."

Nathan continued, "After I left, I started thinking about you and wondering if you have a boyfriend."

I laughed, "Do you expect me to say, 'No?' Of course, I have guys in my life."

There was a brief pause. He asked, "Would you have dinner with me sometime?"

Going into my business persona, I answered, "Sure, give me a call at my office. We'll arrange it."

---

[30] *GQ, originally Gentlemen's Quarterly,* is a monthly men's magazine focusing upon fashion, style, and culture for men.

The next morning when I arrived at the office, a little before nine, my secretary was all excited and announced to the whole office, "Nathan Novak has called for you three times and wants you to call right away."

I said, "Okay," then I took his messages along with several others. I called all my clients first. Then about 10:30 I returned Nathan's call on his private line. He answered, then he told me he was calling to set up dinner.

The next day was Thanksgiving. I was having dinner with my older cousin, Ken, and his family at their house. I had invited my deacon friend, Dave Edwards, to go with me. I checked my schedule to see when I could have dinner with Nathan. I told him I had a week from this coming Friday open, but we should touch base later as WOWT would often send me out of town on short notice, usually the last two days of the week. Nathan and I agreed to touch base later.

Nathan was Jewish as were many of my clients at the ad agency. I learned that they have their ethnic codes that need to be recognized, especially when it comes to women. I knew there was no future to this relationship. I thought Nathan was simply being kind because of my loss of Jay. All my clients knew Jay because when there was after-hours work, Jay was usually with me.

That night, I was cleaning vegetables to take to Thanksgiving dinner, that's the only thing my relatives would trust me to do. The phone rang. It was Nathan. He said, "Did you catch the news? I just received the temporary license for radio KOIL."[31] I want to celebrate with you." Nathan hadn't eaten all day. He was eager to share his excitement and plans.

---

[31]   The oldest rock and roll station in the United States.

I asked, "How did you get my phone number?"

He laughed, "I have my ways."

While Nathan was making a case for a date, I was thinking, "It's 7:30. That's late for going out." Then the memory of Jay and my being alone flashed, again, so I dismissed my initial thought and reasoned with myself, "I don't like this vegetable-kitchen duty anyway, so why not go out? I told Nathan, "I'm in jeans and I don't much want to get dressed up."

Nathan replied, "That's okay. We'll get a pizza or something. I'll be there in an hour or so."

I said, "Let me give you directions."

I learned later that when Nathan hung up the phone, he showered and shaved. Then once he finally got on the road, he lost his way coming over. So, it was longer than an hour before he arrived.

Nathan was driving a VW Rabbit. He looked good; he smelled good; there was a good air about the man. After several tries at getting me into the tiny car, and the electric seatbelt nearly strangling me, we headed for a nearby, roadside steak house. It was a homey kind of eatery with red and white checkered tablecloths. This one was hosted by two older women, identical twins, standing ready to seat you. It was a fun place–or maybe Nathan brought the fun with him. We talked and talked until the restaurant closed its doors for the night.

Boundaries:

When we arrived back at my house, I asked Nathan if he wanted to come in for tea. I explained that I didn't drink coffee so I didn't know how to make it. He said, "If you have the fixin's, I can make my own. That'll keep me awake long enough to drive back to town." It was a thirty-mile drive.

While he made his coffee, I lighted a fire in the fireplace. Nathan drank his coffee, we watched the fire, talked more, and kissed a few times. Then he asked me why I had not remarried in the ten years or so since my divorce. Nathan went on, "You're very attractive, intelligent, you have a beautiful laugh, why hasn't someone scooped you up?"

I said, "Most men think that about me. Then in time, they want to change me. I won't be used, abused, misused, suppressed or controlled: When they try one of those maneuvers on me, I let them know what they're doing. The next time they try it, I'm gone."

Nathan responded, "You're really up front with guys aren't you?"

I said, "I just don't want to waste anyone's time. I don't want to marry. I'm here to explore, learn, and have fun with life."

Nathan asked, "Do you want me to stay?"

I answered, "No."

As I walked him to the door, Nathan told me, "That's okay. You'll tell me when you want me to stay all night with you. I'm not here to pressure you into anything."

I said, "Good." We kissed goodnight. He left.

Thanksgiving with my good friend, Dave, was pleasant, but my thoughts were on the energizing conversation I had the night before with Nathan. I was captured by the joy I found in that communication.

When I arrived home, I found several messages on my machine from Nathan. Within a few weeks, it seemed that most of my other, guy friends just evaporated. Nathan and I were out every night all around the town. We always had something to talk about. Our relationship remained that way throughout the years.

In the second week of December, two of Nathan's three children came home from college. His youngest lived with her mother. Nathan called to let me know his family wanted him to go out to dinner, all of them together. I told him that was no problem for me since I had a tennis date with a client.

After playing tennis, Ruth Humpel and I stopped for a drink. I went home, showered, then I took off my makeup. I was asleep when the phone rang. It was Nathan. He had experienced a night of arguments, finger pointing, and general misery with his dinner partners. He wanted to come see me. I said, "No." I was in bed and I didn't want to get up.

Nathan became suspicious. "You have someone there in bed with you don't you?"

I was quiet for a few moments. I then told him that we had no agreements. I could be in bed with whomever I chose. It was none of his business. He was quiet for a few moments, then he went into a description of his evening's events. Then Nathan said, "Please let me come out; I just want to see you."

I again said I didn't want to get up. He again said, "You have someone there."

I said, "You're right; it's Tex and I won't have this kind of treatment. I'm going to hang up now."

He said, "Okay, okay. I'll call you Saturday. We'll do something in the evening."

I went to sleep to the sound of the television.

The next morning, I decided I didn't need to see Nathan for a while. The phone rang early, but I didn't answer. At 10:30, I knew he would be in a meeting so I called the switchboard and left him a message, just a note that I had called. Then my phone rang every thirty minutes, all day and all night Saturday, early morning Sunday until early afternoon.

I did not answer it. I left home for a while driving to a hill overlooking the Elkhorn River. There I found the time and space I needed to sort through the many things I now had stirred up. About 5:00 p.m. Nathan showed up at my house, but I didn't answer the door. The phone rang Sunday evening until 11:00. It started ringing again at 6:30 Monday morning. Still, I didn't answer. When I arrived at work my secretary announced to everyone within earshot that Nathan had called every thirty minutes.

Finally, I called him. Nathan said, "I've been looking for you all weekend."

I told him I had to do some thinking about me and where I'm going with my life. There was a long pause from Nathan. I didn't say anything either. Then, breaking the silence, Nathan said, "The governor was having a cocktail party and I thought we should go together, but I couldn't find you, and I didn't want to be with anyone else."

I said, "Thank you, but I told you once before what I wouldn't have in my life. Do you remember that?"

Nathan said, "Yes." I wouldn't say he was sheepish, but he knew he had overstepped his bounds.

I said, "We don't need to bring this up again do we?"

Nathan said, "No" There was another long pause, then he said, "Are we on for dinner tonight?

I said, "Okay."

I was always on the move between job assignments, continuing education, and the occasional vacation. Before we were married, I had scheduled and subsequently attended a week-long real estate class in Des Moines. I didn't apprise Nathan of the details of my trip and Nathan did not press for information.

Before I left, Nathan asked if I needed money.

I said, "No."

He asked, "Will you call every night?"

I said, "Of course." That's as far as he dare ask. The pattern and boundaries of our relationship had been established. Nathan never again pressed me for information as to my comings and goings.

Years later, after we were married, Nathan and I were driving from my place to town when the subject of my earlier trip to Des Moines came up. I asked Nathan if I had told him I was going to an appraisal school for the week. He said, "No. I saw you putting your bags in the car. I thought you'd get around to telling me what you were doing sooner or later."

I said, "I'm sorry. I just had a lot on my mind. I had heard it was supposed to be a very difficult course–and it was."

Jay and I always went skiing in Steamboat Springs during the Christmas holiday. I had placed a down payment on a condo the Christmas before and had forgotten about it until I received a bill for the rest of the money. When I told the company of my circumstances, they returned the money. Since I already scheduled the vacation time, I decided to go someplace entirely different. I booked a retreat in Florida, alone, to clean the last of the cobwebs out of my head concerning Jay and then face the challenges of what I was going to do with the rest of my life.

This retreat was Spartan; I didn't have a phone or a TV in my room. That was just what I needed. The third night I was there, a staff member knocked on my door at 2:00 in the morning with news of an emergency call. It was Nathan asking me why I hadn't called him. I said we didn't make an agreement that you wanted me to call every night. Then I added, "It's two o'clock, couldn't you have called when I wasn't asleep?"

Nathan seemed to think I would be out partying or something and just now getting in. I explained this was a mental and spiritual retreat with specific, scheduled times to rise, eat, go to bed, etc. At the end of a long day in training and consultation, one is usually quite tired.

Nathan let me know that he regretted his mistaken assumption. He wouldn't call like that again, but could we agree that I would call him every day, or specifically in the evening. I agreed.

Houston:

About the time my vacation was ending, Nathan asked me if I would be back for New Year's Eve. I said I didn't know, I had to finish some work at the retreat. The work being an individually tailored assignment takes as long as it takes, so I couldn't say for sure when I would be done. "But," I added, "I am close to Houston and I'm going to stop and see Marilyn, my friend and Jay's Godmother, as I haven't seen her for years." The next time we spoke, Nathan asked me her name and phone number so he could call me there. On December 30, I arrived in Houston, rented a car, then I headed for Marilyn's apartment.

I knocked on the door, Marilyn opened it, we hugged; but there in the living room sat Nathan holding a bouquet of flowers. In her thick Texas drawl, she said, "This guy's been waitin' fer you since yesterday—I'm surprised the flowers are still fresh."

I was so surprised and pleased to see him. That was just the kind of unexpected thing no one had ever bothered to do for me. Considering who he was in our community, I just couldn't believe Nathan Novak was sitting there waiting for *me*. WOW!

Nathan explained that he had a hotel room two blocks away. He suggested I might want to make use of it if I wanted to freshen up before we went out to dinner. I said that we probably needed to go there. On the way I asked, "Would you like to have a drink?" He said, "Okay."

In the bar we had time and space to relax and talk. I told him that I knew his divorce was getting increasingly ugly. I didn't want somebody to jump out with a camera and take a picture of us, nor did I want to be knee-deep in his situation as "the other woman." I wanted his word that he was legally separated and that I had nothing to worry about in that regard. If necessary I could stay at Marilyn's place. Nathan said he would never involve me in the mess with his wife. He said many people thought that he and I had been friends before the legal exit of his house, but he had always set those people, and family members, straight. Nathan said, "I was out of the house for months before you and I started dating." With that communication I felt much better.

We had a great New Year's celebration with Marilyn and her husband, Chuck. Nathan was so handsome—and I looked good, too. We were a good-looking couple. We enjoyed ourselves immensely, just the four of us.

Previously, I told Nathan that I just wanted to have fun in the relationship. I didn't want to get married. He said he was really pleased with that because his family was very important to him. If his wife and kids wanted him back, he'd be back in a heartbeat. However, his kiss and hug at midnight, plus his statement, "I love you lady," indicated to me that he might be changing his mind.

When we arrived at the Houston Airport we learned that Omaha was having an ice problem so the flights in and out were stacking up. Nathan wanted us to go to his family retreat in Acapulco, but being the good little employee that I was, I said, "No, I have to be at work tomorrow morning."

The ice eventually cleared in Omaha. We landed at 1 a.m. I finally stayed at Nathan's apartment. It was six blocks from the TV station.

Partnerships:

We continued dating. It seemed as though Nathan had considered me a partner in his life long before I considered him a partner in mine. He had nine brothers and sisters. Most of them were interested in spending the family money rather than earning it. Nathan turned to me discussing several ideas for his businesses. He implemented some of my suggestions for improving employee relations.

Nathan's divorce proceedings seemed as if they would never end. I left work at the TV station and was now selling farms and ranches. I was made for this work as with my background I could craft deals, for doctors, dentists, insurance people, even lawyers, that banks would accept. One of my listings was for a large grass and row crop farm in Central Iowa. It was the perfect investment for three people who were looking for appreciation and tax benefits. The three signed a contract. They also wanted me to buy and manage the cattle for the place. I found the cattle, used my money as down payment, and in ten days the buyers backed out of the deal: I was stuck with a thirty-day delivery date on the cattle contract or I would forfeit my down payment.

Nathan spoke with his contacts about taking on the deal, but he couldn't find anyone interested. Finally, Nathan decided he wanted to do it. After all, his dad and uncle had been feeding cattle for years and Nathan had always wanted to be in the cattle business himself. He put up the same amount of cash that I did, then we borrowed the remainder.

Nathan had such fun with his newfound adventure, yet he had no ability or knowledge necessary to raise cattle and bring them to market. I made the remark that the cattle business was the only business that you could take ordinary income and turn it into capital gains in two years. He couldn't believe it. He was excited. Nathan did his homework and learned all he could about the business. He even went to a state C.P.A. convention to tell them of his findings.

I really didn't care about Nathan's inexperience. I just had four-hundred mother cows with as many calves and fifteen bulls to look after. I had to find places to keep them. I found access to free corn stalks and nearly 3500 acres on a rented a farm. I had over 350 acres for our headquarters, and over 1500 acres of pasture for use in the summer.

I think of our relationship as being a lot like the one portrayed in the movie *Pretty Woman*. Only, I wasn't a hooker, I was a cowgirl. Nathan was the high-powered business man in the fancy suit and limo. To his favor, I cleaned up well. I even owned a collection of diamonds to add some sparkle.

Some of Nathan's family agreed with many others in the area, I was perceived as the "Doris Day of Omaha."

Nathan and I were married March 26, 1979. I was nervous and shaking so badly that Nathan had to hold us up.

We traveled a lot. Every time we traveled Nathan would be busy right up to the day of our departure. If he thought he was not going to make our flight time, or if he thought he just couldn't leave his work, I would say, "Okay, I'll go and you get there when you can."

In the end, Nathan always made the trip. We stayed in the best hotels, wore tailor-made clothes, and we ate at some of the finest restaurants wherever we traveled. Nathan loved good food and attentive service. He was never stuffy, but always gregarious with everyone. Often waiters, even bus boys ended up sitting and talking at our table. Nathan never owned a pair of jeans until I came along; he had tennis shoes to play tennis only. He had never walked on a beach barefoot. We were really from two different worlds, but I fit comfortably in his and I welcomed him in mine.

Nathan won a trip to Japan for two weeks courtesy of the Honda Company. He told me, "I have never spent two weeks with a woman that we didn't end up enemies. If this works for us, I'll be amazed."

I just laughed and said, "I can afford to fly home by myself."

We had so many adventures and laughs. We were like a honeymoon couple; only that's just the way we were all the time, and for years to come. One night while on our way to Japan by way of San Francisco, I met the manager of the Fairmont Hotel. When Nathan joined us at our table, he ended up selling him a car. Nathan's life force was irresistible.

We traveled all over Japan, then returned home through Hawaii and Los Angeles. When we arrived in Omaha, Nathan told me, "If my wife begged me to come back to her and the kids, I wouldn't go now. You are so wonderful. I just love you to death." I told him I loved him, too.

The dust finally settled on Nathan's divorce after three years or so. It had been expensive for him, but that came as no surprise. Nathan ended up telling the judge that he wanted his wife to have 100 percent of the house. In that way, she could use the equity in the property to finance the kids' education, pay for weddings, etc. The kids never knew about the financial arrangements he made for his wife and children; and Nathan never said a bad word to me about his wife. He felt he had to respect the mother of his children, so that's exactly what he did.

A week or so after the divorce settled, Nathan asked me to marry him. I looked at him and asked, "Why?" He was taken back by my response. I continued, "Nathan, marriage ruins a lot of friendships and this one is going pretty good, don't you think?"

He said, "Wanda, I love you with all my heart. I want to give you my name. I want us to travel all over the world and have the same fun we do wherever we go."

I said, "Well, I appreciate all that Nathan, but it's my opinion we might last just six months to a year as a married couple. I think we need to have a marriage built on goals and objectives. Most people marry to acquire a house, have children, promote their careers, or advance themselves socially. We both have all that already. We need a goal or objective that we can work on together, for a lifetime, something that we can't do separately."

It took three weeks, but he came back with a plan to buy a farm, raise our cattle there, and start an alcohol and drug rehab ranch or farm where we would also raise our own food. The plan included a van to take participants to work in Omaha or Council Bluffs. The van would bring them back to the farm in the evening for therapy and life coaching. When the participants were stably rehabilitated, they would return to their city environment. Nathan also planned to have two apartments in the government projects, subsidized housing in both North and South Omaha. Nathan was president of the Omaha Housing Authority for several years so he could arrange that.

Nathan contacted the responsible parties for Omaha's local drug programs. They were ready to send us three-hundred people. He also enlisted all the Omaha Shopping Centers to contribute "x" dollars each month. His selling point was simple: The more drug users we take off the streets, the less shoplifting the merchants could expect. He had raised over six-figures to launch the project.

This was an exciting idea. I loved it, and I loved him with my whole being . . . Yes, I'd marry him!

The Details:

Yes, I'd marry him, however, I had one reservation: I lived without a husband in the house for almost fourteen years. I thought Nathan and I should live together for six months. If our living together worked out okay, yes, we'd get married. If it didn't work out, we would go our separate ways with no hard feelings. I would never have proposed this arrangement had Jay been around.

Let me tell you, that first month was a killer. I knew Nathan smoked, but I never realized how much. I didn't even have an ashtray in my house. He smoked, drank coffee, and played solitaire every morning before facing the world. I bought some ashtrays.

After about two weeks of my cleaning ashtrays every time there was an ash in them, Nathan said, "We have to have a talk." He said he was uncomfortable. He felt like he was in a restaurant where the waiter cleaned ashtrays all the time. So I agreed to back off. Nathan agreed he would step outside for his smokes whenever possible.

Nathan's former wife insisted that he remove all the firearms from their house. I, on the other hand, slept with a shotgun on each side of the bed and a .38 under my pillow. Nathan asked me why I did that. I said it was an old habit from living twenty to thirty miles from the law. In the past I had needed help before anyone could arrive. I felt comfortable in moving the shotguns to the gun rack in Jay's room and my .38 to the bedside table.

After six months, we felt our living together was going well. Nathan thought it was a good time to get married. Again, I had my own thoughts on the matter. I really wanted a happy, no conflict marriage. So, we sat down and went over a list of things that had triggered conflict with each of us and our former spouses.

Nathan and I easily shared chores. I honored most of his quirks. We went down the list arriving at item number twelve. Twelve simply stated that after the two of us discussed the situation and still couldn't agree, the man had the final say. Well, NOW, I had trouble with that one! So we ended up with rule twelve being, the one making the most money would have the final say. I could live with that.

Our final agreement had to do with disagreements. I don't like arguments and I have been known to ask friends to leave my house if they bring in negative vibrations. So we decided if something came up and tempers flared, we would take a separate walk or a drive, then meet at Nathan's office after 6:30 p.m. for the express purpose of restoring harmony. Therefore, the atmosphere at home would stay clean. In all the time we were together, we had three such discussions in his office.

Nathan and I didn't want gifts or publicity so we went three counties away for our marriage license. We invited about four-hundred people to a cocktail party at Harr's Restaurant, a classic small-town Nebraska steakhouse in Waterloo. In the middle of the party, we closed the bar, then we were married.

Living at the lake-house was getting to be too much of a travel burden. I was driving a minimum of a hundred miles or more a day. That put me three hours on the road. Even though banks were lending at sixteen to eighteen percent interest, and timing was not optimum, I put my house up for sale. The house was sold on land contract at twelve percent. That contract gave me an income. While we were looking for a house, Nathan and I moved to Twin Towers. There we had a twelve-hundred square foot, two-bedroom, two-bath apartment shared by Tex, the cow dog, and two cats. That move cut down my travel time, but only by thirty minutes.

Meanwhile, Novak Enterprises was having problems with their twelve auto dealerships' inventory sitting there on the showroom floor at eighteen to twenty-two percent interest, and no one during that period was buying cars. Two years earlier, Nathan had predicted this inflationary period. He informed his siblings. To their chagrin, Nathan suggested they should start living on salary. Ignoring his advice, they carried on spending as usual.

The Freeze:

Back at the ranch, winter came early. Our first challenge came when a $100,000 bull that we were leasing went down. The vet and I applied stimulants, managing to get him up, then into the stock trailer. I drove over seventy miles per hour taking that bull to Ames Veterinary School. He arrived alive; they went to work on him. The vets thought they could save him. The bull stayed in Ames until June when he was needed in the pasture.

Then on Halloween, the sky let loose with snow, big time, and it didn't stop until spring, around mid-April. I had an agreement with a big farmer to clean all his fields with my cows. I had to maintain fences. Then when it came time to farm, I had to remove all the fences. I rented another farm with a homestead that we could use as headquarters.

Mid-November we had a pen of five at the American Royal Stock Show. We won Reserve Champion category. The pen of five sold for $1,700 each. As winter blew on, our losses mounted. I couldn't get that income potential out of my mind. Each time an animal went down, it was lost income.

While Nathan's family did not care for me at all, Nathan's older sister, Sally, and I were somewhat friendly because we shared similar experience in TV. She was the spokesperson for Rosen-Novak Chevrolet. Sally invited us to Thanksgiving dinner with the Novaks, but I missed out because our hired man was taking time off to be with his family.

As the snow piled higher and higher, the cows just walked over any snowdrift that stood higher than the fence that held them in. Now I had four-hundred cows all over the hillside of someone else's property! I chased cattle on foot, through the snow, all over the hillside. (With breathing that cold air I ended up with pneumonia.) However, Nathan surprised me by showing up to herd cattle with his car. That was all the help I needed. (There was no way that Nathan could run.) What a partner! He could sense my need for help and there he was!

Nathan was not handy with the usual chores but he could drive a car and keep the cattle going back into the cornfield while I pushed them on foot from the rear. After they were back in our field, I scattered pellets for them, then I moved the electric fence around the snowdrift securing them where they belonged. Before we left I checked their water. It was okay, so I finished up by putting out their bales of hay. When I climbed into Nathan's car, him in a cashmere topcoat, me in dirty coveralls, I kissed him and said, "You're my angel." He laughed and said he had the better end of the deal because his sister burned the turkey black, again this year. We laughed. I stayed to finished chores at headquarters while Nathan left for town and Twin Towers.

I walked into the apartment coughing and tired. Nathan had stopped someplace to pick up turkey dinner for two. He said, "Take a shower, get comfortable. I will serve dinner." When I walked into the kitchen after my shower I found that he had even lit a candle. What a guy!

Winter set in really hard before Christmas. We brought all the cattle off the fields and back to headquarters. There, feed and water would be accessible. In the rough conditions, we tore transmissions out of trucks. One or both trucks or the tractor would routinely stick in the muck. Cattle fell ill. The cost of feed tripled. We had 100,000 ton of hay laid in for the winter, yet we were running out. We couldn't find any hay for sale in early January. Then the wind chills went down to one-hundred-degrees below zero for ten nights from Christmas into January. We left a truck and tractor plugged into electrical heating and running. They froze anyway. While I was working outside I wore a ski mask and goggles, yet my tears still froze.

Nathan and I had only tree and terrain protection for the four-hundred mother cows and their calves; there were no sheds on the property. The bulls were at another location. We used the barn for grain storage. We sheltered sick animals in two stalls set aside for that purpose. We had to feed the animals corn, as corn supplies heat and energy.

Those were the longest, most exhausting ten days with the weather being so severe. One morning the local dead-animal truck pulled in and took thirty-seven calves that had frozen to death overnight. They weren't sick or starved, they were just caught by the cold laying on the outside of the herd. One of my neighbors put his calves into a metal shed and, even so, one calf froze to death while standing up. I kept trying to convince myself that the thirty-seven lost were just $400 calves, but way back in my mind I remembered the ones at the American Royal Stock Show that sold for $1,700 each. These thirty-seven were from the same bloodline so they held great promise.

To make matters worse, the newborn calves started coming early, particularly to the first-calf heifers. These heifers hadn't matured to calf easily because of the severely cold weather and trouble with rations. Cows won't walk ten feet to water when they don't want to walk any longer on snow. They're the same way with food. Lonnie and I had to literally drive them to food and water when it was sometimes only fifty feet away. No one ever said cows were smart.

One heifer went down to have her calf and it wasn't going well for her or the calf. With Lonnie's help, I pulled the calf from her body only to find the calf wasn't breathing well. I rubbed it down briskly, put some wine down its throat, then put it into the pickup truck with its heater on. We helped the heifer to her feet, gave her a shot of antibiotic, cleaned her, then left her in the barn with water and hay.

With chores finished, I headed back to town. Tex was not fond of the calf occupying a space in his truck, but he tolerated it by sitting next to me. When I arrived at Twin Towers, I enlisted the help of a friend, Liz Grote, to meet me in the basement with a grocery cart and a blanket.

I put the calf in the grocery cart, covering it with a blanket. Nathan and I lived on the ninth floor. I told Liz we were not going to let anyone on the elevator on our way up. Tex was with us. We had to tell only one person to take the other elevator. Up in the apartment, I covered the kitchen floor with newspapers. I barricaded the kitchen doors. I moved a TV close to the front door, then I turned on a Western, loud. If anyone heard a cow, well, they could assume it came from the TV show.

I had frozen first-milk in the freezer. This is the milk that comes first after the animal is born. It is rich in fat and nutrients. It is milked from a cow whose calf was, perhaps, born dead. I thawed some of the first milk then warmed it. While the milk was coming to the right temperature, I supplemented it with raw egg and a small bit of warm wine. I stuck a douche bag hose down the calf's throat and let about a cup of milk flow to the calf. The calf seemed to really enjoy it.

When Nathan walked into the apartment he couldn't believe what he was seeing. Of course, he wondered how I had transported the calf into the building. When I told him he thought that was great fun. I fed the calf every four hours. I slept on the kitchen floor that night. The next morning I asked Nathan if he could help me by feeding the calf every four hours. I showed him the procedure. There was plenty of formula on hand. Nathan agreed.

I went out to the farm to do the chores with our hired man, Lonnie. There would be no more births today. The heifer that had calved the day before was not doing well. We examined her, then gave her another shot. She ate some corn, hay, and drank some water. Her ears seemed to pick up. That's a good sign.

Lonnie and I brought a couple of droopy-eared calves in the barn to bed them down in the warmth. I headed back to the apartment about 3 p.m. It was a Sunday. I was tired. Nathan was in his office downstairs on the first floor of Twin Towers. I stopped in to see him. Nathan thought the calf upstairs was doing well as of the last time he saw it. He thought it was really hungry and he had given it more milk than I told him to give. That didn't sound good to me, but I didn't say anything. I walked into the apartment and stepped over the makeshift gate I had made. I felt the calf, put her head up, she bawled, rolled her eyes back, milk came out the nose and mouth. She died: Nathan felt really bad. I eased his pain when I told him that she was early and her stomach was not right.

Now, I had to smuggle the thing back out. It went well because this time I had Nathan helping me. We left Tex in the apartment. Back at the farm, her mother died, too.

Finally, the weather started getting better. I arrived at the farm one morning and Lonnie told me we had a cow that needed attention. He had her in the catch-pen where the squeeze chute was. I looked at her. Her eyes were bright and her ears were up. I asked "What's wrong with her?" Lonnie said she had a calf days ago and she didn't clean. (Meaning, she hadn't expelled the afterbirth.) I said, "Why did you wait so long?" Then I found out that he'd never cleaned a cow before even though he was raised on a farm and experienced around cattle. (Lonnie was just eighteen.) I told him to go to the house for hot water. I went to my pickup truck looking for a sleeve used for this kind of work, but I was out of sleeves.

When Lonnie came back with the hot water, I had the cow in the chute and my coveralls down around my waist. My right arm was bare. I washed my arm. I covered my hand and arm with antibiotic powder. I reached inside, pulled the afterbirth from the membrane areas in the uterus, and removed them all. Lonnie gave her an antibiotic shot while I put more antibiotic powder in her uterus.

Gosh, when the job was finished my hand and arm did NOT smell good to me. I washed repeatedly there on the farm. Before Lonnie and I went to lunch, I washed that hand and arm with Comet. I just couldn't get rid of the smell.

I arrived back in town early. Nathan was in a dither as we were scheduled to go to an important, political dinner at Churchill's, a well-known French restaurant in West Omaha. I showered and washed paying particular attention to cleaning my hand and arm. I cleaned the cuticle. I doused my hand and arm in perfume.

Finally, I dressed. I walked into Nathan's bath and asked him to smell my hand. He said, "It smells like perfume."

"Are you sure?" I asked.

Nathan said, "I'd tell you if it wasn't okay." When I related the story of cleaning the mother cow, he fell back on the bed with laughter. I didn't think it was all that humorous. Perhaps he had an insight on what else was going to happen that night.

We arrived a little late at Churchill's. The owner greeted us. Appetizers were already being served. He kissed my hand: I held my breath: Nathan was about to split a gut. I shook my head, "No." As we were walking to the private room, Nathan kept asking, "Can I tell 'em, can I tell 'em?"

"No, no," I said, "a thousand times no! I would be so embarrassed." Then, as we entered the room the host who held a very high position in state politics walked over to us. He, too, kissed my hand.

When Nathan was about to burst into laughter he developed a visible vein that ran from between his eyes straight up to his hairline. Believe me, that vein was about to burst!

Nathan, with his love and appreciation, was a great partner for me. I was comforted in the feeling that he was going to stick with me, maybe because I was so different from any other woman he had ever known.

No Relief in Sight:

Across the nation, economic times were not good, with no sight of it getting any better. Novak Enterprises had to go into Chapter 11 bankruptcy to reorganize due to the twenty-two percent cost of keeping inventory while nothing was selling. The Novak family fired Nathan at the age of fifty. Imagine going out for your first job at fifty. Nevertheless, Nathan was hired on his second interview at Merrill-Lynch. He studied and worked hard to pass his securities license exam. Merrill-Lynch gave him only one chance to pass.

Once licensed, Nathan worked long hours just like at Novak Enterprises. His family was upset, it seemed, because he could secure a good job and be successful. While Nathan was making his career transition, he was also having to deal with the Internal Revenue Service regarding Novak Enterprises. The IRS had Nathan sign an agreement to pay them "x" amount of dollars each month to cover the last quarter of withholding taxes on employees.

Physically, Nathan was feeling poorly with no sign of improvement, so we went to the Mayo Clinic to find out what was happening with Nathan's body. Apparently, he had a case of undiagnosed polio when he was a kid. It seems the body was tired of working certain muscles for such a long time. He was having difficulty with one leg and he was not able to walk very far. Apparently, Nathan was a borderline diabetic also.

The cattle business was starting to come out of the doldrums. Calves were being born. Our leased bull, Black Gold, was back from Ames and he had sixty heifers to look after. I figured after Black Gold was finished with his "girls," I would turn in Woolly Bully to finish the job.

In mid-August we found Black Gold in a stream, lying down, and he wouldn't stand up. Lonnie and I used a hoist to lift him out of the stream. The rescue seemed to go well, but when his feet touched ground, Black Gold dropped dead. The postmortem revealed the lower quarter of his liver had exploded. The vet who worked on Black Gold at Ames was now working for our local vet so he was familiar with the bull. He said that the problem was likely the same thing that was wrong with him before. It was no doubt the result of pushing a young bull to championship confirmation too fast, typically accomplished with drugs.

Early fall, my bank was sold to an investment group from Nebraska. The new president was young and lacked experience. He would speak with Nathan, but ignored me, literally turning his back to me as he spoke with Nathan. Nathan, however, was again my champion. The banker probably figured that Nathan was a car salesman, thus he didn't belong in the cattle business. Working with the banker was difficult for us because I was the one who understood cattle and farming, not Nathan. Nevertheless, they agreed that Nathan and I should not be in the cattle business, so we sold everything in the early fall.

I was tired. I hated failure, but you just pick yourself up, dust yourself off, and start all over. I went back to selling real estate. Nathan moved from Merrill to Shearson; he liked it a lot better there. He didn't retain any hard feelings because of our joint experience in the cattle business. I would not have expected him to; he wasn't like that at all.

If Nathan had a personal fault, it was that he just wouldn't pay any attention to his diet, his medication, or his health. While on the road selling real estate, I always managed to be downtown so Nathan and I could lunch together. Not only did I always enjoy his company but this was a small chance to see that he paid some attention to his diet.

I had grown tired of living in the apartment. I wanted another house. I was still enjoying an income from the sale of my lake house. Interest rates had dropped, so the new owner was in touch with me; he wanted to pay off the land contract.

Meanwhile, Nathan was in a fight with the Novak family and the trustee of Novak Enterprises' bankruptcy. The reorganization plan reduced Nathan's thirty-one percent compensation to one half of one percent. He sought to find out why and how this could be justified as he had been solely responsible for paying off the IRS and other old bills. This really upset him.

With the $25,000 left coming from my lake house we bought a Frank Lloyd Wright Protégé-designed house called Thunderbird House because of its style. I named it simply, The Bird House. We put it in the name of a friend so the IRS couldn't attach it. It was a wonderful house, but the first owner didn't take care of it; it needed a major overhaul. We managed to have that done.

Even though Nathan's original agreement with the IRS was in writing, the IRS changed its demands. After he started making more money, Nathan's monthly payment doubled: Then the IRS tripled its demands. None of the changes were in writing. In April, Nathan had a bad month at Shearson so he couldn't pay the triple payment in May.

On June 6, a Monday, IRS agents showed up at Nathan's office; they zapped our bank accounts; then they appeared at our home. I wasn't there.

Nathan was a proud man. He struggled to be responsible for Novak Enterprises' but neither his family nor the IRS offered any help having placed the entire burden on his shoulders.

Nathan had been putting on seminars in small-town Iowa to procure more business; I had been helping him at that. I was working on the next seminar when at 4:30 he said he was going for lunch. I told him I'd stop by where he was eating before I went to the Sylva Energy Circle.

I went by about 7 p.m. Nathan had been drinking on an empty stomach. His food was just coming. I asked Nathan if he wanted me to pick him up after the Energy Circle. He said, "No," as he'd be all right after he ate. I went to the owner-bartender and asked him to call me if Nathan was in no condition to drive, or call him a cab. He said he would do one or the other.

I came home, went to bed, fell asleep. The phone rang at 1 a.m. I would have been out the door straight away to pick up Nathan but he said, "Wanda, I'm in jail."

My heart sank.

I asked him, "What should I do?" Nathan said he needed $500 to get out. I asked, "Where should I get it?" He said go to his office; in his desk he had some American Express Checks. So I went to Nathan's office. Boy did I have to do some explaining to the night-watchman. Once I had the checks, I couldn't find any place open to cash them. They wouldn't take them at the jail. I called a friend, Liz. She worked at Omaha National Bank in collections. I picked her up at her house in the downtown area. She drew money out of her ATM. I gave her the American Express checks, then I took her home. At the police station, I paid Nathan's fine; he met me outside the jail.

I didn't say much on our way home; neither did Nathan. When we arrived back at The Bird House, he told me that he had wrecked the 1967 Buick Wildcat that I had restored. He knew that I dearly loved that car, but I told him it was just a car and it could be fixed. I asked if he was coming to bed, he said, "No," he had to figure some things out. I thought he was thinking of his career. He knew the media would have a field day with his DWI.

When I awoke at 7 a.m., I could see Nathan hadn't come to bed. He had been drinking coffee, smoking, and playing solitaire since we arrived home at 4 a.m. I asked if he wanted breakfast, he said, "No, but could you bring me my check books?"

I said, "Okay." I went to his office and found the check books. Then I took them to the library where he was sitting.

I asked Nathan what was he doing. He said, "I just want to sign some checks for you."

Instantly, I knew what he must have in mind. I took all the clips out of our firearms; I hid all the ammunition. Then I used up all the gas in his car, going places not too far from the house. When the gas gage registered past empty, I brought the car back home.

I called my minister, Colleen Leines. She and her husband, Beryl, dined with us frequently. This time they came over specifically to speak with Nathan. I also called another friend of Nathan's to come over, a professor who taught psychology at Creighton University. Nathan charmed his way through the conversations. He knew exactly what to say to all of them.

He was upset with me for having brought these people in to speak with him, but Nathan didn't say a whole lot more. He went to bed in the evening, right after having some food. The next morning he was back to playing solitaire, smoking cigarettes, drinking coffee. I asked him if he'd like to have breakfast with me. He smiled for the first time in two days, "Sure."

We talked. Nathan told me about the IRS, his family, and how he just didn't feel well. I told him we could declare bankruptcy. The IRS would have to leave us alone. I could help him at his office. He could go to the Mayo Clinic where he had the best chance of getting his back and leg fixed. Once he was feeling better, he could work from home. I could be his legs, going to the office and running errands for him.

Nathan also told me what had happened to his twenty years of work for Novak Enterprises going down in percentage. I assured him that we could manage without them. Nathan told me how sorry he was about wrecking my car and the DWI. He knew how much that sort of thing bothered me. He said he felt he had not been a good husband, not for the past two years as he had been throughout the earlier years.

I asked, "Have I ever complained?"

Nathan said, "No," and my lack of complaint bothered him, too.

I assured him that I loved him; we married for better or worse, in sickness and health. We were just experiencing one of those down times that we committed to pulling through. I felt confident that, together, we could come out of this on the other side, better and stronger than ever before, "Because we're partners." With that said, Nathan left the table. He said he was going to clean up. As he walked up the stairs to the bedroom suite, he said something else over his shoulder, but I had my back to him and didn't hear.

I showered, then dressed. Before I left for work, Nathan had cleaned up and I found him sitting in his home office. He asked what my schedule was for the day. I told him. He said he was going to stay home from work. I told him I'd be home to fix him lunch either at 12:30 or 2:00 depending on what I was able to accomplish at the office downtown.

I called Nathan after every meeting, but he didn't answer. I thought, "He's not very happy with himself right now so he probably doesn't want to talk." We didn't have caller ID. On the way to the trainer where our dog, Cat, was being worked, I had just a moment of hope that Nathan was home and didn't do anything foolish. I was so thankful when I opened the garage door and his car was in the garage.

I drove into the garage, then I closed the door. I let Cat out. I walked around the back of my car. I thought, "I'd better get my exhaust checked; there are a lot of fumes in here for having just driven in."

I opened the garage door leading into the house. At the end of the hall I saw that the door there was shut. We never shut that door. I stopped, then looked toward Nathan's car. Funny, it looked like the headrest was broken. I walked over to the driver's side and there I couldn't believe my eyes.

I touched him and I knew he was dead. DEAD. All of his magnificent life force was gone.

I was surprised . . . No, I was shocked, so shocked I recoiled onto the cold steel of my car. Now, as I write, I can still feel the touch of it on my back.

For a moment, time stood still. It was like being surrounded by a bad, inescapable dream . . .

I just looked at what remained of Nathan in disbelief.

Denial ran through my mind. I reasoned, he was happy at breakfast, wasn't he? We had such a good talk. I thought the crisis was over.

Then some things he said much earlier flashed through my mind: "I love you, Wanda; I would never want to hurt you or embarrass you.

"It took fourteen years for my dad to die and my mother visited him every day at the hospital. I would never put someone I loved through that."

Nathan's older brother, Mike, had attempted suicide while he was in the Vets' Hospital. It was a failed attempt. Nathan's reaction was, "That damn Mike never could do anything right."

Well, my love, it looks like you wanted to do this right. You've always wanted to do everything right. I ran your car out of gas, you just filled it up. Could I have helped you more? I don't know. You're gone. Now I'm alone again. What should I do?

Then reality started creeping into my consciousness. *What do I do?* I've not dealt with a situation like this before.

I went into the house. Trey, Cat's dad, bowed down in front of me; Cat went to him. He stood up, put his muzzle in her ear, then they both ran into Nathan's office. There they jumped on the couch and rested with their chins up on the back of the couch while they stared at the garage door. I dialed Eunice, one of my best friends. I told her what happened. I asked for advice. She said call 911. Still in shock, I said, "Okay," and then I made the call.

The paramedics arrived within five minutes. I put the dogs in the fenced backyard as they had a tendency to protect me and suddenly there was a house and yard full of strange people. I went around to Nathan's chair and there on the desk I found his suicide note. I walked out to the garage where the paramedics were trying to revive him, but he was cold. I said, "I found this note he left." The paramedics immediately stopped their rescue attempt. They called the police. Now there were even more people around: The police, a fire engine, paramedics, neighbors, friends, all started showing up.

Man I had to think. What to do from here? Jewish people are buried the next day. I called Nathan's Rabbi in New Mexico. I told Rabbi Kaiser what had happened. He said he'd be on the next flight to Omaha. He called in advance from New Mexico to arrange for use of the Council Bluffs Synagogue across the Missouri River in Iowa. I told him Nathan wanted to be cremated; did he have a problem with that? He said, "No." However, later we found Nathan's family did have a problem with that and Rabbi Alan was there to fight that battle for me. My cousin, Eunice Corbett, lived in Iowa, about fifty miles away. She drove over to help me. Eunice and I cleaned the house–although *she* did all the work. Then the food started arriving.

Nathan's Rabbi briefed me on what the widow does in a Jewish funeral. Then he told me that he was a priest in the Jewish faith and he had never performed a funeral or a wedding. I said that was okay. I knew Nathan would want him to do his service. Later, I found out that Nathan had spoken with Rabbi Kaiser about the service during the previous Thanksgiving holiday.

I sat in the front row of the synagogue. Nathan's two daughters sat behind me. His son wouldn't come from Chicago. Nathan's brothers and sisters, along with their spouses and children, were next. The building was filled to capacity. The community hall was filled as was the street in front of the synagogue. I performed my wifely routine; then I took my seat. My minister gave a eulogy about a tree in the forest. I can't remember it all.

After the prayers, Alan stepped to the podium and said, "Nathan Novak killed himself." (Oh, my god, you could hear a pin drop.) Then he added, "If you are asking why, then you were part of the problem." This statement was directed at certain family members.

I felt eight psychic knives in my back. Alan ended his talk with reading the poem, "For Whom the Bell Tolls."[32]

No man is an island,
Entire of itself.
Each is a piece of the continent,
A part of the main.
If a clod be washed away by the sea,
Europe is the less.
As well as if a promontory were.
As well as if a manner of thine own
Or of thine friend's were.
Each man's death diminishes me,
For I am involved in mankind.
Therefore, send not to know
For whom the bell tolls,
It tolls for thee.

As the reading finished, the church across the street started ringing its bell. Though not planned, I thought the timing was perfect.

---

[32] Words by John Donne: The passage is taken from the 1624 Meditation 17, from Devotions Upon Emergent Occasions and is prose. The words of the original passage are as follows:

No man is an island, entire of itself; every man is a piece of the continent, a part of the main. If a clod be washed away by the sea, Europe is the less, as well as if a promontory were, as well as if a manor of thy friend's or of thine own were. Any man's death diminishes me, because I am involved in mankind; and therefore never send to know for whom the bell tolls; it tolls for thee..."

With Alan's help, the house was set up for a minyan[33] to help Nathan move on with his spirit life. Even with the rabbi there, no Jewish people showed, not even Alan's family or children.

The rabbi announced the itinerary at the synagogue, that lunch would be available immediately, followed by the minyan to be held every night. Some of our non-Jewish friends started showing up for lunch. We broke out the Mumm Champagne, Nathan's favorite. He had put it away after our wedding to be used at another special occasion. This seemed appropriate.

The Champagne flowed. People started telling stories about Nathan. Some were humorous, some were appreciative of how he had helped people when they were in trouble. Nathan's style was just quietly showing up with a check or some other assistance.

One man told how his wife was diagnosed with M.S. They had two children ages eight and ten. He said that Nathan arrived unannounced at his office one morning. Nathan said, "I heard your wife is in a bad way." Bob, we'll call him, said, "Yeah. I'm just trying to figure out how to handle this with the kids and all." Bob went on to relate how Nathan offered his company plane that was equipped for a wheelchair. Nathan would have the family flown to the Mayo Clinic, "Where they have real doctors." Then Nathan handed him a check for $10,000. Nathan asked, "Will that help you?"

Bob said to Nathan, "Thank you so much, but I can't pay you back."

Nathan replied, "Did I ask you too?" Nathan turned to walk out. When he reached the door, Nathan turned to look at Bob. Then he said, "I'll call you on your trip to Mayo."

---

33 Minyan, a group of ten males, 13 years or older, required for conducting Jewish public worship.

Another married couple reminded me of the night we went to their house for dinner. While we were waiting for dinner to be cooked, we were having a cocktail in their new, enlarged living room with windows all across the back. Sharon was telling us about this new recipe she was trying with wild rice and chicken. She explained the recipe called for not cooking the rice first and, "That's why the delay."

Just as she finished her explanation, we all heard a large pop and a bang in the kitchen. Jumping to our feet, we went to see what the noise was about. We crept up on the oven where Sharon was slowly opening the oven door. There was rice and chicken all over the oven. As we stood there looking over the scene in surprise, Nathan popped up with, "That's what I call wild rice!" We all laughed; Nathan suggested, "How about pizza?"

The day following the minyan, we took Nathan's death certificate to the IRS collections agent, Mr. Wilson. It's amazing how you remember the name of a really suppressive S.O.B. I told him to collect from someone else. Nathan was no longer able to pay him anything. Wilson just looked down. The IRS saw fit to audit me six months later. All they could find was that they owned me more money. However, two years later they placed a $225,000 judgment on Nathan. They are now paid off.

Nathan was born in Nebraska City. We took Nathan's ashes to a farm there; it was the first farm his dad bought after he came to this country. Nathan's uncle had a cemetery on the property. He has since petitioned the state of Nebraska to secure approval for a dedicated cemetery on that farm.

Jewish tradition says you don't put up a tombstone for a year. However, there was a lovely grove of tall pines just north of the cemetery. Nathan never liked the hot sun, so that's where we scattered his ashes, in the grove. It was still a hot location though the wind did cool it somewhat. I also put a handful of Nathan's ashes in his yarmulka along with a piece of jewelry that he loved. That jewelry kept disappearing on us, but it turned up the night after Nathan's funeral in the middle of the dinning room floor where I and many, many people had walked all day long, and none of us ever saw it.

That evening, again, friends showed up; the Champagne and stories of humor and appreciation started to flow. Everyone was laughing when I felt an itch between my breasts. I reached down my blouse to scratch it. There was grit there. When I brought it out, I said, "Oh, my gosh, Nathan's ashes!"

For a few seconds it became very quiet in the room. Then Alan said, "Well, Wanda, wasn't that his favorite place?" The laughter started back up followed by more stories.

A year later, Nathan had his tombstone with my declaration fixed in stone:

You were loved.

From each event in my life I learn something. I learned from these few special nights with friends that it is much better if you're going to remember the past, to remember the good times, the fun times, the unique times. People can get stuck in severe losses. When they do, their own lives can take a serious turn for the worse. I guess with my philosophy on death, I know that death is just a moment in all time. Physical death is a ruse. I believe in life, and the infinite spirit.

Alan stayed around for about a month. He visited all his parishioners at the Council Bluffs Synagogue. I went back to work in real estate selling a million dollars in property in six months at an average price of $57,000. I helped start the brokerage firm of Kidder & Novak. I supplied the money and list of clients. Kidder supplied the license and experience.

Following Nathan's death, I secured some more life coaching from a wonderful man in Denver, John Galusha. He helped me address guilt and remorse that I couldn't shake by myself. He helped to validate the positive aspects of my relationship with Nathan. He made me aware that I had talent and ability to help others with life coaching technologies. We wrapped up the coaching with John assisting me in setting a course for my future.

I should mention that when things get tough for me, there are three women I mentally turn to as role models. Two were real people having lived through their own challenges. One is a fictional character.

First, there's the "Unsinkable Molly Brown."[34] She faced the challenge of rising from poverty to aristocracy. Once she arrived she was never accepted by the aristocracy, but she went on to a life of philanthropy.

Jackie Kennedy-Onasis, need I say more? She suffered her husband's blood on her clothes and his dead or dying body cradled on her lap. Through her ordeal she continued to be composed and brave for her children, her country, and her husband's family.

Auntie Mame, no matter what happened to her she always saw the brighter side and pursued it with all her energy.[35] No matter what happened, forward was her only direction.

---

[34] Margaret Brown, born Margaret Tobin (July 18, 1867 – October 26, 1932), more widely known as Maggie Brown or Molly Brown, was an American socialite, philanthropist, and activist who became famous as one of the survivors of the sinking of the RMS Titanic. She became known after her death as The Unsinkable Molly Brown, although she was never called Molly during her life. (Wikipedia)

[35] Auntie Mame, fictional character from a 1955 novel by Patrick Dennis that chronicles the madcap adventures of a boy, Patrick, growing up as the ward of his deceased father's eccentric sister, Mame Dennis.

Lastly, the Creighton Professor told me that she thought Nathan was fine during their last conversation and she questioned, "Was there something wrong with [me]?" I didn't see nor hear from her for months. When I finally did she said she had been wrong and just couldn't face me.

It was over: My best friend, my lover, my confidant, the one that I could laugh at and with . . .

For me it has been a long, terrible void, without Nathan. Yet, I know that when one phase of life ends there is always a new beginning.

Nathan was a man of tradition. He broke family and religious upbringing to include me, a non-Jewish person, as an equal partner in all respects.

It's been twenty years, I still miss him, I miss his laughter, I miss the good times, the bad times, and the many adventures we shared.

> *You can kiss your family and friends good-bye and*
> *put miles between you, but at the same time you*
> *carry them with you in your heart, your mind, your*
> *stomach, because you do not just live in a world but*
> *a world lives in you – Frederick Buechner*[36]

Notes:

---

[36]   Frederick Buechner, Presbyterian minister, American author.

Pliability

*Only when you can be extremely pliable and soft can
you be extremely hard and strong. – Zen proverb*

The *American Heritage Dictionary* defines *pliable* as: 1. Easily bent or shaped, 2. Receptive to change; adaptable: *pliable attitudes*, 3. Easily influenced, persuaded, or swayed; tractable.

A strange thing happened on the way to the forum . . . No, no, that's another story—I mean to say on my way to an appraisal. I usually drove from 65,000 to 110,000 miles a year most of my driving career, only a couple of times landing in a ditch, but having no accident with another car.

I was sitting in my van at one of the three traffic lights in Missouri Valley, Iowa. The sky had been sprinkling rain and the concrete road had enough moisture on it to make it a little slick. I had just pulled my seat belt loose so I could reach something on the dash . . .

I heard the screeching of tires from another vehicle, then a thud and a crunch at the back of my van. The impact moved me towards the car in front of me, but I didn't hit it. The driver came out of his car as if I had hit him. When he saw that I didn't, he asked if I was okay. I thought I was okay, so he drove on.

The person who hit me from behind had considerable damage to her car. The hood was bent to such a degree that I don't think she could see to drive even if she had wanted to. She wanted to call the police.

All I could think of was being late for my appraisal appointment. The police arrived to examine the damage to both vehicles. We provided details for the police report, then we all went our separate ways.

When I arrived at my scheduled appointment, I took one step from the van, and fell down. My depth perception had changed. If I turned my head too fast, my eyes would not keep up with the movement. I immediately saw the first of three doctors. He was a chiropractor. I submitted to X-rays, then began a treatment plan.

I have always been quick to heal; but when I failed to get over these symptoms I went to see another doctor. He was an M.D. He sent me to a hospital for a brain scan.

The first M.D. sent me to another M.D. He specialized in fixing vertigo. While one therapist was working on my eye coordination, another therapist was working addressing the vertigo situation by retraining my brain.

Time passed without much, if any, change in my symptoms. Whenever I went to bed the room would spin. If I walked from the bedroom to the bath at night, I saw and felt as if the house was a ship on rough seas.

Three hospitals, three doctors, three therapist and three years later, I was not much better than the day of the accident. They were now trying to retrain and rewire my brain to solve problems with my physical phenomena. I had always healed in a hurry and this condition was a nagging puzzlement to me. Why was I not healing?

I spoke with the doctors about the long term situation and when did they think all this would be handled? I was spending valuable time with these people. I wanted my condition to return to normal. I wanted to be healed so I could get on with my life. The answer I received was, "Maybe in two to five years." Good grief! I am not a patient person! I can't deal with "maybe" in a situation like this.

Eunice, bless her, is a free spirit and good friend. As a matter of curiosity she is always investigating alternative studies, treatments, or therapies. She found a place in Dallas that boasted of some new technology, some mental-spiritual healing processes. One day while we were talking she told me about it. She lent me a couple of their books to read. I read the first one, it made sense. I called to order that book and some others. I had given the doctors and physical therapists three years to work their magic, but not much had changed. Maybe my difficulty wasn't physical. I was not only willing to look at alternatives, but I was anxious for some relief however I might obtain it.

I started correspondence with these people in Dallas. Building up a mutual degree of trust and respect, I set aside two weeks and $5,000 for training and travel expenses. Soon, I had loaded my dog, Cat, into my van along with clothing and trail food. I headed for Dallas. Cat was a good travel companion. She stayed in the open van and when I let her out for air she never strayed far from the van or me. We checked into a motel late on Sunday.

Monday morning I met my coach and confidant Eric Wollery. I started the program right away. I spent several hours a day in study and perhaps fifteen to forty-five minutes each day, one-on-one, with Eric.

My turnaround was almost immediate, although you will likely find that hard to believe: After just seven hours in private consultation with Eric, my vertigo was gone, the constant pain in my shoulders and neck had vanished. I walked out of the last session not having to have my hand on a wall for steadiness. I went outside to let Cat go for a run. There I twirled around in circles with arms outstretched; I didn't fall over. My head and eyes were coordinated and functional as they should be. It was a miracle!

I can tell you now what had happened three years earlier: The night before the accident I was relaxing in the hot tub with my significant other. He had a cigarette in one hand, and a beer in the other. (I neither smoked nor drank alcohol in those days.) He had recently become a "born again" in the faith in which he was raised. He took this moment to announce that God had spoken to him. God told him that he had to leave me because I was evil.

That's the damnedest thing I'd ever heard. I was instantly rigid, not pliable. I saw, in my mind's eye, a giant wrecking ball that nearly knocked me out of the hot tub. In the microsecond that my mind raced looking for a rational explanation, I wondered if he would leave if I were incapacitated and couldn't support him and his son. In that instant I dismissed the thought, but the shock and confusion of the moment stuck with me like some hidden baggage until it cleared three years later. When the significance of this moment came to full view, the incapacitating heaviness of the injuries along with the physical pain all vanished!

I returned to Omaha and my work, pliable, free of pain and vertigo.

Fascinated by the techniques they used, I returned to Dallas over long weekends to take classes on their techniques. I wanted to learn all that I could. Between my appraisal work during the week and my studies on weekends, I went through a period of remarkable, personal expansion.

I took a job with an Omaha-based company whose function was to place critical weather and market information in the hands of ranchers and farmers. This was done with computer links, local radar, and satellite connections. With my experience in ranching and farming, I was able to move right into step. Soon, I was blowing the lid off a four-month pilot sales program.

I was producing more than the combined efforts of the other three salespeople on the program plus I was putting my field reps and myself in bonus each pay period. The company executives took to observing me at work. They couldn't figure out what the magic was. They asked me if I knew what I was doing. I told them, "Yes." They asked me to train the others. I said, "Okay, but I need $3,000 in cash and $3,000 in stock." They objected for the simple reason that they couldn't justify the expenditure because they couldn't understand the process even though they appreciated the results.

When their pilot program closed, they transferred me into another department. There I successfully applied the same techniques. My heart's desire was to teach, to help others be more successful. The things I learned in Dallas were the perfect tools. However, I needed to know more.

When I gave my notice to the company, they asked why I was leaving. I told them I was going to school in Dallas. Before my final day, they asked me if I would stay with the company if they created a territory for me in North Texas. The offer was tempting, but I knew how much time it would take to create that territory, so I declined. I told them how much I appreciated the offer but the study program I was going to do would take my full attention. I couldn't honestly do both. (I have never burned any bridges where I've worked and I've often returned just to say, "Hello." I am always welcomed.)

Again I loaded up Cat and clothes. This time I also loaded a small refrigerator, a microwave, and an exercise machine. Then I headed off to Dallas for several months of uninterrupted study and personal enhancement.

My original plan was simple: train in Dallas then return to Omaha where I would start teaching. The people in Dallas showed me a different vision. I had knowledge of public relations and advertising, a strong work ethic, and access to startup capital. They had the techniques.

My primary motivation is always to help others be more successful. That's how I sell; that's how I teach. To accomplish my new goal, I studied for about five months approximately ten to twelve hours a day, five days a week, often eight hours on Saturday. Sundays I took off to clean, handle domestic chores, and perhaps see a movie.

I was flattered when they invited me to join the team. I returned to Logan, Iowa, put my house up for sale and, six months later, sold the farm as well. There was no hurry to sell the farm as it was producing an income.

Knowing myself as I do, I knew I wanted to be part of a team, yet maintain my independence, so I created my own corporation in Texas, Powerhouse Unlimited, expecting to work in close cooperation with my new associates.

The kickoff for my consulting business came the weekend of the New Business Expo at the Dallas Auditorium where approximately eleven-hundred new businesses displayed their wares. Over three days we contacted probably fifteen-hundred to two-thousand people. We handed out all of our business cards, all of our brochures, and issued five-hundred or more Life and Skills Analyses. The analysis, when graphed, gave a person a good look at fourteen different areas of their personal management style and success potential. About two-hundred profiles returned to us, most by fax. Out of those contacts we filled four different classes in communication, sales techniques, finance ("more money"), and relationships. We had about thirty students in each class. We were invited into twenty-five or so corporations to speak. We registered fifteen managers for private coaching. It was a heck of a kickoff!

I hired a public relations firm and through their connections we secured write-ups in *The Dallas Business Journal*. The P.R. firm arranged introductions to special business clubs, women's organizations, political organizations, etc. The P.R. person was an old pro. She taught me how to introduce myself using a series of personal "commercials," ranging from ten to forty-five seconds. I learned that in Texas a woman offers her hand first if she's going to shake hands. At events and meetings, I learned to put my name tag on my right shoulder so that when shaking hands the tag would fall in the line of sight of the other person. These are seemingly simple things, but all the little things add up to success.

Two of my students came aboard my company to help. We arranged speaking engagements at some of the men's business organizations. They made presentations to potential customers. We established an Internet presence with the help of Bill, one of our students, a graduate of Texas A&M, through his startup Internet company. I started attending leads meetings and Chamber of Commerce events, the Dallas Chamber, the Black Chamber, the North Dallas Chamber, Metroplex, Addison, and Plano Chambers. I settled down putting all my attention on the Plano Chamber meeting because Plano was considered to be the Silicone Valley of North Texas. They were a very personable group; Plano seemed to be a Mecca for new businesses as well as the old guard.

I noticed that the Chamber Ambassadors physically welcomed every new business in the area, so I became an Ambassador.

Twenty to thirty of us would comprise the welcoming committee. The Ambassadors also involved themselves in numerous, charitable events. The second year of my involvement in the Ambassadors I was nominated as chairperson. I accepted. As chairperson I organized and scheduled all the Ambassadors at their assigned civic events for the year. I chaired the monthly Ambassador's luncheon.

Besides the work and long hours involved with the Ambassador role, there were benefits. For example, I was invited to sit with the Plano Mayor and Chief of Police at the Black and Blue Ball, a charity event for children. Following that event another door opened and I gave a presentation to the Police Officers in Plano.

Everywhere I went I left a business card, a brochure, and a favorable impression. Earlier I spoke of personal presence; this I would call business or commercial presence. We were happening!

I worked about eighteen hours each day which seems like a lot, but you know if you are doing something you really enjoy, time doesn't matter. Time, in that regard, is totally unimportant in my reality. It goes back to *Purpose*, being in the right place, at the right time, working with the right people, doing the right things, things you love. For me it all came together in a big way.

I could tell you many success stories connected to my clients and students but I'd like to tell you about the one experience that I am most proud of. It involves *pliability*, youth, and teaching:

My assistant, Beverly Miles, placed a display booth at the Women's Expo. There we met with a high-school principal from Dallas. It was a long process, but we eventually scheduled a training class in communication. According to the principal, the chief problem with her students was in communications. My associates provided most of the training. I arrived on the last day to find a room full of kids rolling their eyes. I suppose the response was because of the way I was dressed: I was wearing an extra-large Texas Ranger baseball shirt, blue tights, and tennis shoes. I carried a red-plastic, child's baseball bat, and a broom. The students were slumped over in their chairs. Though my instructors weren't slumping they, too, were rolling their eyes when they saw me. I instinctively knew that what I had planned to say wasn't going to work so I shifted gears (*pliability*), scrapped my plan, and held a dream session.

The class was 85 percent Hispanic, 10 percent Black, 5 percent White. All my life I've been taught to look another in the eye, to acknowledge that there's someone there, to always be honest with them. I was set back when I learned that the Hispanic males were taught from childhood by their fathers to look in people's eyes and lie. The girls were taught by the mothers to never look people in the eye. There were no such difficulties with the Blacks or Whites. The instructors had to deprogram the boys, that being one of the biggest challenges in the whole class. Our goal was to have the students look another in the eyes for twenty minutes because that was deemed the length of an average conversation. The girls had difficulty reaching one minute. We eventually coached all the girls to fifteen minutes of *presence*; a few even reached twenty.

During the training I was astonished to find that the girls wanted to have a baby just so they would have someone to love them and someone they could love.

I began the dream session: "Have you ever dreamed?"

The disinterested response was like, "What's that?"

I posited, "If you had all the money in the world, what would you want to have in the way of a house?"

The students went through some open communication, talking out loud with each other, then they came up with a home with two bedrooms, one bath. With some coaching they came up with another answer, "Three bedrooms, two baths, and a two car garage!" They were really pleased with themselves. I said to them, "Come on guys, you have all the money in the world. That's a small house."

The vision started growing. Now it was twelve bedrooms and twelve baths. I said, "What if you are cooking in the kitchen and you have to go to the bathroom?" Such a situation had never occurred to them. They added a bathroom off the kitchen in a laundry room and a bathroom off the card and pool room. We were now at twelve bedrooms and fourteen baths.

Then we continued to build the dream adding a swimming pool with a pool house, including another bath therein. Someone wanted to fish, another wanted to be able to ski. With the addition of a lake the total area of the house and property grew considerably. The property grew large enough to land a plane and one young man wanted room to raise a goat and two pigs. We were now at one-hundred twenty acres. Then we talked about cars and trucks.

The students started with a Mustang hardtop. Then it had to have lights on the bottom, it was metallic blue, a five-speed, and that was changed to a convertible. Then they decided to have both hardtop and convertible. Then a fleet continued to grow to include pickup trucks, Cadillacs, sports cars, and so on so we added a fourteen-car garage and automatic car-wash to the dream house.

All the time I pointed out to the students that there were no ultimate right answers that everyone had to agree to but there were right answers for each of them. Once the right answer was attained, it would have to be detailed and pictured in the mind.

Then I pointed out that to have all that we've been visioning, a person needs money and I think that was the first time in their lives they started looking to the future. Then we discussed education, career, and where the money would come from to realize their dreams. I also had them look at what would stop them and the greater percentage said, "Family" or "Peer pressure." Not one of them said it would be themselves that would bring the dream to a halt. I focused on that and we had a private conversation between the kids and me on how they might stop themselves. I felt it was free, open communication, kind of like brainstorming in business, and they would never be made to feel wrong as far as I was concerned. I think the freedom of expression was something very unfamiliar to them at school and at home. They were so enthralled that they were standing on their seats and moving towards me during this whole exercise. The discussion became a competition: In the excitement one would want to do or have something bigger or greater than the other. Even the girls started to participate.

When I saw the alloted class time ending I started to talk about what I really came to talk about: I wanted them to know that I, though being just one person, truly believe in them and they can have anything they want in life. They could drop out of school, end up pushing a broom or digging a ditch; that would be okay with me. That was the purpose of my carrying a broom into the meeting. I wanted them to open up their thinking. They could have a rewarding career and earn enough money to have their dreams become a reality. They could be anything they chose, doctor, engineer, teacher, maybe a player for the Texas Rangers or other professional sports team, or they could just be financially free to take the entire family to a game and pay for all of it without concern.

I let them know that if I, at my age, could obtain what I wanted in life they certainly could, too, but they would have to plan and work for it. With their young, healthy bodies they would have an easier time than me.

I really had to be pliable to walk in there and know that what I was about to do was not going to work unless I did it a different way.

171

Notes:

The Early Years

Pioneer Spirit, Pluck, Grit:
Leadership By Example

It was a Friday. I know it was a Friday because my dad was at the Livestock Auction in Norfolk, Nebraska when he received the call. He attended that sale every Friday for most of his life. I was but fifteen months old at the time. As unusual as it may seem to some people, I have my own memories of this experience; these memories were later supplemented by what others told me over a period of several years when I was old enough to understand.

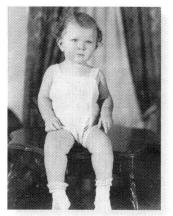

Me at one year.

As I recall, Mom and I were going to visit Grandpa Harker, her dad, her twin brother, Melvin, and his family who lived in Iowa. She had borrowed Granddad's car to make the trip. The car was a big, black, 1935 Buick sedan, much bigger than our Model A roadster that Dad was driving. I was excited about taking the ferry that would carry us from Decatur, Nebraska across the Missouri River to a dirt road on the other side where we would continue to Onawa, Iowa. It was a small ferry that carried only one, large vehicle, sometimes two small cars. Mom had to watch me closely because the previous time we used the ferry I threw my shoes in the river. Mom always bought expensive shoes so

Dad and Mom at their wedding.

this was no small loss. When she was a child, the shoes she wore didn't fit properly. As a result, she had funny feet. As a child, I thought they were funny feet, but maybe they were just a little deformed from cheap, too-small shoes she wore when she was young. Anyway, Mom was not happy when my shoes went overboard, so I was spanked once we were alone.

It was August and farmers were putting up hay. I could see them from the car. We were driving down a gravel road heading east of Walthill, Nebraska. I remember standing on the front seat with my hand on Mom's shoulder. Mom pointed out the Oak Leaf Schoolhouse that would soon be coming up on our right, resting between two steep hills. At the time, the north side looked like a cliff to me, but later I was told it was only a fifty-foot embankment to a flat, hay meadow below the road.

Mom continued to talk about our visit. She mentioned that Dad would pick us up on Sunday, but my thoughts were on the ferry ride. A tractor-trailer hauling cattle was coming toward us. Later I would learn that the truck passed us and the rear of his trailer hit the rear of the heavy Buick. I remember the car heading for the schoolyard, then when Mom moved her feet to the pedals the car veered to the other side of the road. She fought it, but the car went sideways and the guard railing came up over the front of the car. The truck did not stop.

I can still see the rolled down window on my side of the car. It was rolled down so I could put my hand out in the breeze, my hand but not my head. The window broke. I can see and feel my body rolling all over the front seat of the car as if it were not so long ago. At the time it seemed like we were moving fast, but now I think it was more like slow motion. Mom was trying to hold me and control the car at the same time. The car rolled over and over. I was almost thrown completely out of the car, then back in.

When the car came to rest I was on the ground outside of the car. The roof of the car was cutting across my middle. The lower half of my body was out of sight. The ground felt cool. I seemed to be pushed into the ground. It felt like something was under my legs so they were up. There was no pain.

The dry, August, Nebraska dust surrounded us, and maybe some smoke, too. Mom was trying to turn the key off. Mom smashed her head through the windshield. She received a cut from between her eyes, up her forehead, on to the back of her head above her spine. She carried that scar with her for the rest of her life. I'm guessing the steering wheel had damaged most of her ribs. Later I was told most of them were broken. Yet my mom was always tough. She was talking to me not knowing where I was. "It's okay, Honey, I've turned off the key. There won't be a fire." She climbed out of the car. She was looking for me; she followed my whimpering even though she was bleeding profusely.

When Mom found me, she tried to pull me out from under the car. I held my arms up to her, but when she reached for me, blood would come out in clumps. I screamed, covered my face, and attempted to pull away–but I couldn't move. I can only imagine the terror she was going through. She repeated her attempts at pulling me out from under the car, but to no avail. That '35 Buick was just too heavy.

I clearly remember two men in big, faded overalls come running up. I would now suppose they were running as fast as they could run. They wore felt hats. I noticed the hats because I needed something familiar to hang onto. Dad always wore a straw hat at this time of the year.

The men tried to get my mother to lie down to stop her bleeding. At the same time they attempted to move the car off me. No one knew what my wounds were because they couldn't lift the car up enough to pull me out. They looked for a piece of wood to use as a lever. With the help of a passerby, a young man, the three men managed to lift the car off me, then they helped Mom and me up the hill, then into the young man's truck.

In those days almost every town had a doctor of some kind. The young man drove us to Walthill about five miles west of the accident. There would be a doctor there. We arrived. The truck stopped. I remember the young man easing out from under my leg as he got out of the truck. He was gone momentarily. Mother remained in the truck with me lying across her lap.

The doctor came out, looked at us, then stated that he was neither qualified nor equipped to help. My mother, who was always in control, told him to get some bandages out here for me and her if for no other reason than to keep the dust out and the flies off the wounds. He did do that much.

The young man climbed back into his truck, backed out of the parking place, then headed out of Walthill to Pender where we lived. Pender was and still is a small town, but it did have a hospital. Mom had worked there about four years earlier. It was fourteen miles away, fourteen miles of Nebraska heat and dust, then through town and up to the top of the hill where the hospital was located. The young man said he couldn't believe how quiet both of us were. He kept looking over to see if we were dead, I suppose.

When we arrived at the hospital they rushed us into the operating room.

I heard my mom in back of me saying, "You can clean me up, but don't do anything until she's taken care of. Do you understand me?" I recall that she was in the corner of the room on a stool. Two nurses were working on her.

Please understand, I could hear everything that was going on and, later as they operated on me, I could see everything, too, from a perspective high up in a corner of the room. Materialists would say that this is just an illusion, a part of the brain playing tricks on itself. Spiritualists would say this is the spirit, the very being itself separate from the body. Either case being the true explanation, I'll just say it was a profound experience that set me off on a positive course for the rest of my life.

They took off my clothes, then started to clean me up. Two doctors were there, an old one with white hair and a young one with black hair. I did not recognize the younger doctor. I trusted the old doctor as Mom had taken me to him before. He was gentle and kind. The doctors couldn't believe the condition of my leg. "Why hasn't she bled to death?" "How is it she didn't have any broken bones?" At the time I didn't really know what the concern was as I was well separated from the body and feeling no pain.

I had a small cut on my left leg and they pulled out a couple slivers of glass. (The cut formed an "N." As a kid I would later joke and say I was branded "N" for Nebraska.) Then they turned to the big job, my right leg. The old doctor said, "It looks like her leg just turned around maybe on some broken glass or a piece of steel. The bone is chewed up a bit, but everything is cut in the leg, skin, muscle, tendon, veins, arteries, and nerves. It's a miracle that the wound was clogged with dirt, gravel, grass and weeds, or she would have bled to death. I don't think she's lost even a drop of blood from this wound. This is going to be a job. I don't know if we can save the leg . . . and then there's the possibility of infection . . . It just doesn't look good. God, how am I going to tell Mildred this?"

The young doctor said, "We need to cut it off. There's so much damage and it's been without blood for so long, it won't grow. It'll be a stump and if infection sets in . . . it needs to be off."

I could hear them discussing the situation. Mentally and spiritually, I'm screaming . . ."Sew it on! Sew it on!"

Finally the old doctor said, "We're going to sew it on. We can always cut it off. I'm going to go over and talk to Mildred. You prep her."

Mom was in the corner of the room while the doctors were quietly discussing their course of action. My body was sleeping. The old doctor walked over to Mom. She asked, "What's going on?" Mom had worked at the hospital as an anesthetist. The old doctor said, "Mildred, we're going to try, I said try, to save the leg, but we may not be able to do it."

Mom looked into his eyes, put her hand on his and said, "Save that leg. I know you can."

The next thing I remember is waking up in a large crib in my Mom's room; it had wheels on it. Now my leg hurt. It throbbed. Oh, how it hurt. I didn't know if I could stand the pain. At the time it seemed like I wore a large bandage with tubes sticking out. Dad came in. At one time he had broken ribs himself so he knew he could do nothing but hold Mom's hand and reassure her that she would be all right–and so would I. He said, "Whatever it cost, we'll go to wherever to get her fixed."

Later, my Mom's sister-in-law came to see us. She had come from Iowa where we were headed when the accident occurred. She said it was too bad that your daughter would be "mutilated for the rest of her life." After she left, and for months thereafter, my mother would hold me in front of her face, then tell me "You will be fine.

You are beautiful." That's called programming today. Then, it was just Mom's determination and pioneer, survival spirit.

It took me a while to learn to walk again. Mom wouldn't let me baby my leg or even think that there was anything wrong with it. My leg was cut, nothing serious, and it was healing now. Soon it would be as good as new. Everyone repeated that mantra to me, Grandpa and Grandma French, uncles, aunts, cousins, the hired man . . . everyone. Dad said he would get me my very own puppy to chase when I was healed to the point that I could run. True to his word, when I could run beside Dad, he took me to a friend who had a littler of bulldogs. I picked out a spotted one. I called him Tousey O'Socks, O'Socks, O'Socks.

I think Mom was haunted by that scare until the day she died. She told me when I was older she would have plastic surgery done on the leg. The leg was fully functional and the scars meant nothing to me. In my early teens when I was figure skating, I made it to Nationals three years in a row. I landed all my jumps on that leg. I finally told Mom, "It's working fine. I don't need to have any surgery that might mess it up. I want to just leave it the way it is. Now I've grown proud of it." Thanks to all concerned, the outcome of this experience is but another miracle event in my life.

Now move forward twenty-five years for the rest of the story. I was attending a horse auction, standing there wearing a short skirt. A man approached me. He said he knew no one who could have a scar like that, taking note of my leg, unless . . .

He started his story with, "I was a fifteen-year old and had not been driving all that long. I stopped on the road to see what had caused the damage to the guard rail as it looked fresh." He left his truck to see how the banister was damaged when he saw the sight below. He came down that hill in "leaps and bounds." He told me that when he reached the bottom of the hill everything he saw made him so scared he just squatted down with his back to the top of the car, then jerked up with all his leg strength. He alone raised the car enough so the other two men could pull me out. Only then did they see the cut on my leg.

He told me that he had a dirty handkerchief and Mom told him to put it over the wound as flies were gathering on the scene. The three men managed to escort Mom and me up the hill, then into his truck. He said they all knew "she was hurt inside," but she stayed on her feet asking them stop occasionally so she could "catch her breath," or so she said, but they all knew it was the pain holding her back. Yet she didn't indicate any sounds. Mom had to be in pain; she had tears rolling down her cheeks, but said nothing, nothing except she wanted to know where Wanda was. How was she doing? Was she hurt? Was she bleeding? The young man carried me in his arms. The two other men helped Mom ease into the passenger's side of his old pickup. I was placed between them with my head in Mom's lap and my legs resting on his leg. He told me he stayed around the hospital leaving only when someone told him that we would live.

I can tell you everything about that operating room: the tile, the color, the relative size of everything in the room, where Mom was, where I was in the room relative to everything and everyone, and so on. I could see it all. During the experience, I just kept getting proof that I was not a baby body but uniquely myself, a spiritual being. Thereafter, I had no preconceived restrictions that some people have when being just a body. Bodies are restrictive, spirit is not. I also realized somewhere in my being that if this body died I could always secure another. This is likely where I picked up my lifelong distrust of doctors, as they apparently didn't know everything they needed to know to help a person, the whole person, not just the body.

I did make a promise to myself then that I would always take care of my mother no matter what. I guess it looked like she really needed help. I fulfilled that promise several times over, particularly when I was an adult. After that accident Mom became very physical with me. It seemed like I was spanked everyday whether I needed it or not. Dad never knew about the spankings. I didn't tell him. He found out for himself one day when I was fourteen. Mother struck me in his presence; I was never again hit after that.

I also wanted to be beautiful for my mother. That seemed so important to her. So my second husband saw me just two times without makeup over a twelve-year period. It's interesting how decisions made under duress can affect one's life thereafter, both positively and negatively.

Notes:

More on Principles:
Time For Church

I have been told that I could speak in clear sentences by the time I was eighteen months. When I was four I announced to my folks that it was time for me to go to church. They seemed surprised, but Mom said it was, "Okay." She asked me which church I was going to. I said I thought Methodist. She asked me how I'd get there. I told her I could walk; it was closer to home than the swimming pool and the park.

Wanda French at 4 years.

Now neither my Mom nor Dad nor Grandpa nor Grandma went to church. However, Dad's sister and all her kids went to church as often as twice a week, at least. Now as I look this event over the only place I can figure out why this idea of going to church would come to me would be the four or five family funerals I attended with my folks in the previous year or so.

The preachers doing the services talked about "Sin," that we were all born sinners. They said we had to "know God," and "God" had to know us. I wondered how would he get to know me if I didn't go to his house? They said, "God" had ten rules to live by. Well, I didn't know these rules. I thought I would learn them, and in that way, get to know God at the same time. I didn't really want my folks to know that I was so dumb that I didn't know these things. I thought that when you were born you should know this stuff. So going to church seemed like the best way to get all this important information. This is how my young mind was working.

Ervin French. Studio portrait of my father taken when I was 4.

The first few times I went by myself. Dad seemed to have business to attend. He would walk me just partway, or maybe he went to the grocery store, the one that his best friend owned; it was only two blocks away from the Methodist church.

Mildred French. Studio portrait of my mother taken when I was 4.

While I had always perceived my childhood adventures and excursions as self-determined, solo activities, I now know that Mom or Dad always had someone watching over me. The first time I went to church by myself, Johnnie Myers, the man who owned the grocery store, came out to sweep his sidewalk just as I was walking by. He told me to be careful crossing the street a block away as that was a State Highway. In those days I always believed that I was alone and fully responsible for myself. I think that was a good lesson courtesy of Mom and Dad.

I attended church there with the Methodists for almost a year. When I started kindergarten some of the kids went to the same church so I had some instant friends in school.

I was even in the church Christmas program. At home our kitchen was about twenty feet long. Mom would have me stand at the south end while she was doing dishes with her back to me, she at the north end. It was Mom's expectation that I deliver my poem loud enough that I could be heard at the back of the church. We practiced in that kitchen over and over.

When Mom and Dad came to the program they were the best-dressed couple there. Dad always dressed well, as did Mom, unless he was in the fields. Each day he wore tan pants, a white shirt with a tie, a Stetson hat, and boots. I was so proud of them that night and so happy that they came. On the way home we stopped at the local liquor store for a toddy. I think, perhaps, Dad must have wrecked the car or it broke down because we walked home that night. Dad seems to have wrecked a number of cars in his lifetime. It's strange what you can remember from when you are very young. I really don't know why we walked home, but I do know there was moonlight, snow, and people singing Christmas carols. We sang along, too.

Later in Sunday school the next year, after Easter service, the Sunday school teacher and her daughter made fun of me because I didn't have an Easter bonnet. I pushed her daughter out of her chair, then I walked out. I didn't go back to that church ever again.

The next week, I went across the street to the Presbyterian Church. There, they were all old folks; they had no Sunday school. I waited a week or two, then I went with my neighbors to the German Lutheran Church. There they spoke German so that didn't work for me. Next was the Holy Rollers. Finally, I went to Midnight Mass with one of Mom's friends. There, I connected because I liked the discipline and pageantry. I wanted to join that church, but Mom said if I didn't marry a Catholic I might be in for a lot of trouble, so she wanted me to wait. It's a good thing I didn't join because my first husband was an atheist or an agnostic depending on the day and his mood.

I went to church to learn the principles of good behavior and conduct in this life. In the long run I realized I was taught best by example from my parents and grandparents. Oh, Mom and Dad had their faults, but if anyone needed help they were there with assistance; they each conducted their lives this way until they died. Dad was there with money, Mom was there with free nursing or food or both. When Mom died, I found at least twenty charts for people to whom she had administered morphine; these would be people in our community who had suffered from cancer. According to her charts, she usually cleaned them for the local mortician, too.

When Dad died, I found at least fifteen I.O.U.'s among his things from men who, in their time of need, had borrowed money for one thing or another. These men would never have been able to repay him, but Dad lent his support nonetheless. My parents never went to church except for funerals and weddings, but they regularly gave more than a ten percent tithing to their neighbors, friends, and strangers.

If I complained about something while in Dad's presence, he would step close to me and say, "Look around, sweetheart, there's always someone worst off than you, so don't complain; do something about it."

My reality is that a person should give back in time, money, and energy. That's not time *or* money *or* energy, but *all three*.

Notes:

True Grit:
Presence, Persistence, Pliability

It was a time of celebration, my sixth birthday. My mother's sister, Jean, and her husband and three children came to celebrate. I was never taught to address my mother's and father's sisters and brothers as Aunt and Uncle; I don't know why.

My folks married when they were in their late thirties, later than their brothers and sisters, so all my cousins were considerably older than me. They were nine, eleven, and thirteen.

Me at age 5, on stage singing "God Bless America" at the Nebraska Veterans Annual Meeting, Norfolk, NB.

We had the usual, predictable fried chicken, potato salad, and birthday cake. Towards sundown the adults decided we should go to the public park to play on the new equipment; it had just been installed that spring. To us kids the most important piece of the new equipment was a double slide. It was situated so the parents could watch over us while they drank spiked Coke or 7-Up. The park was lighted; it was about 9 p.m.

We kids decided to race around and on the slide. It would be a team event. The eleven-year oldest girl, Donna Jean, and I would be playing against Jackie and Gary. The idea was to start on the ground at the bottom end of the slide, crawl up it to the platform on top, cross over to the other side, then slide down. When both team members were up the one slide and down the other we would run to the double stairs. That team would win. What fun!

The new slide was really big compared to the old one. There were two sets of steps going to each side of the slide. Each slide had two humps so one could really go faster than the old slide. I'm now guessing it was about twenty feet high. There were two large half hoops that helped people to hang on when sitting on the slide ready to go down.

We all walked through the pattern so everyone knew what he or she had to do. My cousin, Gary, yelled, "Go!" Up his side of the slide he went. I was first to go up for our team. Gary reached the top before me, he ran over to come down the slide towards me just as I reached the top touching the safety hoop with one hand. Gary hit me coming down. I went over the side and to the ground. I don't think I screamed because Gary carried me to the parents. He said, "I think she broke her back," because I was in a contorted position. My Mom and her sister were both Registered Nurses. Mom said, "I don't know about her back but that arm is in bad shape."

Gary laid me on the ground. Mom and her sister started examining me. The light from the streetlights and the lights from the car made it bright enough to see. Dad and Garland ran across the street where the familiar, old doctor lived. He had recently retired. It was an emergency and the old doctor obligingly said, "Bring her in."

They laid me on the dining room table. They gave me a shot of something. I fell asleep. When I awoke I was upstairs in bed at home. Oh God, I hurt. My whole right side felt heavy. I could hardly lift my arm; it was so hot. I called for my mom. She jumped up and came to me. I told her what was happening. My fingers looked like little sausages. The badges were cutting into my fat fingers. I begged Mom to please cut the bandages. She did but there was no relief. She rocked me all night. She said, "We'll get this X-rayed as soon as we can in the morning. Just hang on. I know you can handle this. Just try to sleep." I was so hot. It felt like my arm was burned. I drifted in and out of sleep with really weird dreams that were like a strange movie.

Mom was always there for me when I was really hurt. I don't think she slept all night either. There was never any hugging or kissing in my family. I was never told that I was loved. Yet, I was always aware that both Mom and Dad were dependably there for me.

Mom's relatives stayed over night. I wasn't hungry. I just wanted to get to the doctors office. Mom and her sister thought something was not right and they, too, were eager to get me there.

Doctors were different in those days; they made house calls working throughout the rural community. They were often in the office early, particularly if there were no rounds at the hospital. The old doctor had called the young doctor and so had Mom. This is the same young doctor who wanted to cut my leg off earlier. However, he was the only doctor in town and we were at his office early. The X-ray showed both bones in my arm were broken on the diagonal. They weren't set properly, so they would have to set them again.

The doctor and his nurse were going to do this procedure in his office. I begged Mom to come in with me. The doctor told Mom there was no need; it was a small room and we would be only a few steps away. He turned to me with assurance that Mom would be just steps away.

I remember fighting the mask being placed on my face. I always hated the mask. The doctor was trying to talk to me and calm me down. I remember everything going black, then I was floating outside the building. I was moving toward what we called the "dredge." The dredge was a stream that had been dug so it could handle more water thus cutting down on the flooding in the area. It was the size of a small river.

I arrived at the bridge to see the dredge filling with water. Water rose to almost the bottom of the bridge. There I saw strangers urging me to come across. I started across the bridge, but stopped in the middle. It was still dark as in a bad thunderstorm. Water in the dredge was getting higher and higher. Just as it started over the banister to sweep me away, the water turned into bubbles. There were bubbles, millions of bubbles everywhere. Then, the bubbles seemed to burst all at once. In that instant, I was surrounded by the brightest of lights. There were bright circles of energy everywhere, but there was no other being to see or communicate with me.

While this description of the event is as I experienced and remember it, my aunt later told me that back at the doctor's office, the young doctor walked into the waiting room where she and Mom were sitting. He announced to my mom, "I'm sorry, Mrs. French, we did everything we could, but your daughter died and we couldn't bring her back."

Mom leapt to her feet, grabbed her sister's arm, then pushed the doctor out of the way. "Oh, no she's not!" she shouted.

They ran into the room where my body was lying on the table. Mom pushed the nurse out of the way, knocked the mask off my face, and went to work on me. Mom and her sister took no caution with my body so my arm was broken again. They took turns working on me. Mom was shouting at me to come back.

Where I was in essence, it was like I wasn't wanted there in the bright light. I looked around and it didn't seem to me that I should be there either. Then I had the distinct sensation of falling backwards, past everything that I had just previously floated by. However, now it was like a race backwards. I slammed so hard back into my body that my mom said my whole body lifted off the operating table as I gasped for air. My eyes popped wide open.

Then I went back to sleep. They reset my arm with no more anesthesia. I slept most of that day, then on into the evening. The relatives were gone by the time I woke up. My cousin left me not saying he was sorry. I had no hard feelings. After all it was a race. I just lost to a bigger, stronger person. I didn't really think ahead before I agreed to the game. I would be more prudent next time.

We didn't see much of the relatives after that. They moved to Colorado where Uncle Garland was to become an important engineer and help design Aspen Snowmass. Cousin Jackie and Aunt Jean eventually died there. Cousin Gary went off to be a forest ranger and, I believe, cousin Donna Jean died in some mysterious way. I heard these things in family gossip but never saw those relatives again.

This all happened in June. When they took the cast off in August my arm was crooked. My hand went at about a forty-five-degree angle to the left. This time Mom went to an orthopedic surgeon in Sioux City. He said they would need to do surgery, perhaps put in two clips, but the arm would be straight. So we went to a Catholic hospital where the nuns who were nurses wore grey. Again, I remembered begging them to please let me go to sleep. They put the mask over my face. I was not quite asleep when I felt the mask go on, but I didn't protest too long or loudly.

When I awoke my first response was to get out from wherever I was. Mom and a nun were trying to calm me and get me under the covers. I told the nun, "Lady, you have the funniest looking clothes on of anyone I've ever seen." Mom was mortified; she scolded me. The nun said that people had said worse things to her before. In spite of their restraint I tried to crawl on my hands and knees away from them and out of that hospital. Now I don't know what I would have done had I escaped, but then it did not matter.

While we were struggling a priest walked into the room. I had never seen him before and I doubt he knew me. Observing the situation he said in a loud voice, "Young lady! You get under those covers right now! Go to sleep or we'll take you right back to where you've come from!" I don't know what he meant by that. Maybe they were going to send me back to the original sin they had talked about in church. Nevertheless, I responded.

Mom told me this story later. She said I sat on my knees with my arms pulled up like a puppy dog. She told me I turned, put my body under the covers, pulled them around my neck and went to sleep.

The doctors took the last brace off just before Thanksgiving. I can still write left-handed if I have to, and I've had to several times in my lifetime.

Going thru death and coming back with an awareness of the event gives one a feeling that one can accomplish anything.

Notes:

Motherly Advice:
Principles, Passion, Purpose

Our house was on the southeast corner of Pender. When you stepped out into our backyard you were in our pasture and outside the city limits. Ahead on the other side of the fence was one of our row-crop fields. To the left, the pasture went about a block to Grandpa French's orchard. When you left his orchard you were in the part of the farm that had all kinds of buildings and feedlots. So we were very close to being in the country.

Me in my scout uniform and Tousey

I was but seven years old, in the second grade. There were no girls in my neighborhood but there were seventeen boys. All but two or three were cousins. Most of the time they hung out at Christianson's house, two blocks from our house. I had to walk by their place on the way home from school. The boys often gathered there with their Chow dog. My chicken bulldog would meet me every day about half way home from school. The boys would urge the Chow to attack Tousey. Usually it was an ear, leg or throat that would be in their Chow's mouth. Then I would get in a fight with the boys and the big boys would push me around.

This bullying had gone on for several weeks. I had even attempted to walk home a different way. Tousey would go his usual way, I would hear the fight then run to his aid. I recognized three of the boys as being in my class at school.

Mom was preparing supper when I came into the house upset and dirty. I was getting water to clean Tousey of the mud and blood. She asked what I was doing? I said, "Cleaning Tousey, I'll be back." (Dogs were not allowed in the house or car unless there needed to be an emergency trip to the vet or something like that.) Animals, no, people, yes. Remember, my Mom was a nurse. You could perform surgery anyplace in our house, but not on animals.

When I finished, I put Tousey in the milk-house on a bed of old towels and a blanket. I gave him a pan of water and another dish for scraps from the table.

I was still frustrated when I came back into the kitchen. There I was skinning out of my school clothes and getting into my chore clothes. Mom started asking questions about my obvious, frustrated look and Tousey's condition.

I remember telling Mom that she needed to call the school so they could keep those boys after school. Then I would have time to get home without a dogfight. I thought she should call their parents to have them stop their kids from picking on Tousey and me.

Mom kept peeling potatoes. In a few minutes she said, "Wanda, I am not here to fight your battles. You must learn to fight your own battles and handle your problems. You need to outthink the mob or the bully."

I started to justify boys, their size, too many . . .

Mom interrupted me. "Wanda, what you need is an equalizer."

"What's an equalizer?" I asked.

She asked me, "When those boys go to school, what do they carry their lunch in?"

I answered, "Paper bags."

She asked, "What do you take your lunch in?"

I looked at my metal lunch box with a new thermos inside, then I looked at her. She was smiling that peculiar little smile she had.

There was my purpose and plan for after school. I was not going to be a victim anymore! When the odds were what they were, why fight fairly?

The next afternoon, I came rushing into the kitchen all smiles. I put my lunchbox on the counter top. It had several dents. Mom looked but said nothing.

Mom was mixing meatloaf for supper. She asked, "Have a good day?"

I answered, "Yep," and went into the living room to listen to my stories on the radio.

"Change your clothes," she ordered.

Figuratively, I became one of the boys after that day. They never picked on me again. Sometimes they defended me from others when we all participated in football, baseball, and soccer on the streets of the neighborhood.

Notes:

Grandpa French:
Presence, Persistence, Principles

My folks rarely left me with a baby sitter. If they had to go someplace where kids weren't allowed and they couldn't get anyone to stay with me, Grandpa French came down. It was in the fall as I remember, the air was cool. We hadn't yet put the winter stove into the living room. (Can you imagine, putting stoves into the house in the wintertime and taking them out in the spring?)

Grandpa and I were listing to the radio. He was in the rocking chair. We were laughing about the program. I think it was a show called "Fibber Magee and Molly."

I heard a very calm voice coming from Grandpa. A very present, calm, voice said, "Wanda I need you to boil some water for tea right now." I was sitting on the floor close to the radio. I looked at him. Something was wrong. I jumped up and ran to the kitchen. I struck a match, lighted the gas stove, then checked the teakettle. It had some water in it so I put it on the lighted burner; then I went back to the living room.

I saw him put a small pill under his tongue. He also had a "medicine bottle" in his hand. He always carried it in his shirt pocket. I knew something was very wrong and I knew he had heart trouble.

I was close to panic. I was eight or so. I thought, "What else can I do? Do I need to call someone? Go to Mrs. Eickler? What?" Grandpa was still calm. He asked, "Is the water warm yet? Get a cup and put the water in it even if it isn't hot, just warm." I pulled a cup down from the cupboard and poured water from the teakettle. It had steamed so I knew it was warm enough. I took it to him. He poured about half of the contents from the bottle into the cup then stirred it with his finger. He blew on it, then he sipped a bit.

"Grandpa, what can I do? Call a doctor? Call Mom and Dad? What?"

He said, "Nothing, child. Just calm down. It's just a little heart attack. We've done about as much as we can right now."

I was frantic; I didn't know what to do. I felt so helpless.

Grandpa said, "Just turn off the radio and we'll talk."

I jumped up, turned off the radio, and returned to the floor by his knees; I sat there hugging mine.

He was so present with his pain, so calm. "Honey, I've had these before" He never called me that before. "We never know what might happen. I may die or I may live." He said, "You almost died a few years back when you were with a doctor and a nurse." He went on, "You remember when my brother Seth died 3 years back picking corn on this farm. Remember when your Mom and Dad had his body in the bedroom?"

I said, "Yes."

Grandpa went on. "He didn't have any attacks like this, he just died. You know, Wanda, it doesn't make any difference where you die or when. I think it's all decided when you come into this world when you'll die. It doesn't make any difference if it's just you and me, if I'm in a bed surrounded by my family, or if I'm all alone someplace."

He asked me, "Are you afraid to die?"

I said, "No, not really."

He said, "Neither am I" He smiled and then he said, "That hot water you fixed and my whiskey did the trick. You did a good job. I'm going to be okay now." Then he winked at me and said, "We don't need to worry your folks with what happened here, do we? It's just between us."

I told him I'd keep his secret.

He put forth one of his principles regarding life and death to me that night. I guess I've kept it and I continue to confirm it in my thoughts.

It may be interesting to you when he died. He was visiting a sister-in-law in South Dakota. The pilot light on the furnace had blown out. When they were found, his sister-in-law was still in her bed, peacefully gone. Grandpa had left his bed making his way as far as the kitchen, just short of the door out of the house by about two feet. It looked as if he fell after catching his foot on the leg of a kitchen chair. Essentially, Grandpa had died alone.

Notes:

When Nature Calls:

*Look around Wanda, there's always
someone not as well off as you. – Dad*

Recently someone asked me what it was like to live in a house with no running water. It's like this: If you have never had something, but otherwise made do, how would you know that thing was missing?

As a child you are taught how to survive by the people with whom you live, how to make do with what you have, and how to do without. When I was a baby, say less than a year old, Mom bathed me each day in one of her dish pans. Her large teakettle

Eighth grade graduation picture.

served to heat the bath water. She cooled it to baby-temperature with hand-pumped drinking water. We always had a bucket and ladle in the kitchen for our drinking and cooking water.

Saturday was bath night for the family. When I outgrew the dishpan, I bathed in Mom's laundry rinse tubs. In the winter, big buckets of water were brought to a boil on the cook stove and cooled with drinking water out of the drinking bucket. In summer, water was often simply heated by the sun. The tub would be filled from the pump in the early morning and then we'd bathe outside in the evening.

I usually bathed first. If, when I finished, the water wasn't too dirty, Mom would just add hot water for the next person. I had to be in bed by 7 p.m. so that's why I went first. It seems like we were cleaner people in the winter compared to summer. There was a tub for everyone in the house; the hired man usually had something to do on Saturday night, hanging out with the boys, playing cards, or whatever, so he would take his bath first, after the dishes were washed, but before Mom, Dad, and I took our turns.

There was a sink in the kitchen but no plumbing. We dumped the wash-water down the drain that ran out the house and onto the ground. There was no septic tank; the gray water just went into the garden summer and winter.

During the week we took sponge baths. There's a technique to it. You start with your face and work your way down using soap and water, one part of the body at a time, rinsing and drying as you go along. You have to always be figuring out how much hot water you will use and how to mix in little dippers of cool water so you don't use up all your hot water before the bath is finished.

Bathing was not our most important use of water; it seems other things had priority: coffee, tea, cooking, dish washing three times a day, separator for the milk and cream machines, washing clothes, etc. These things were more important than bathing. There was never any place for dirty dishes to pile until the end of the day; they had to be cleaned after each meal. There was little cupboard space for pots, pans, and china. Paper plates were a rare-seen luxury. Water had to be pumped for the chickens, too. Every time you needed water for drinking, cooking, or cleaning it had to be pumped and carried into the house.

Now what to do when Nature calls? Our outhouse, like everyone else's, was cold in the winter and hot and stinky in the summer. In really cold weather we could use a pot in the house and carry its contents to the outhouse, but water had to be pumped into the pot to clean it. No matter what, the pot had to be cleaned.

I learned to carry out a plan when nature called: wake up and go to the outhouse; go again at school just before classes finished for the day. That way I could get by with just two trips a day to the outhouse. When school was out for the summer I made a trip early in the morning, then again late at night as the offensive odors seemed less at those times.

When I was young I had nightmares of falling in the outhouse hole or being attacked by wasps. I would have to run out with my britches down, but that never happened in real life. Having indoor plumbing was a luxury. It didn't matter if it was on city property or at a friend's house, I looked forward to using those facilities.

I never thought there was anything wrong with not having a bathroom. Several families that lived close by had outhouses, so I was never ashamed or felt less because of it. It was a normal way of life then in that area. I was twelve when we put running and hot water in the house. What a luxury!

Notes:

Planning

*In preparing for battle I have always found
that plans are useless, but planning is indispensable.*
— Dwight D. Eisenhower[37]

This final chapter is really what I want to talk about because this is where all the tools in the Life Skills Toolbox come together. This is how an idea or a dream or a vision manifests as reality.

The Century Dictionary defines *plan* as a formulated scheme for the accomplishment of some object or the attainment of an end; the various steps which have been thought out and decided upon for the carrying out of some project or operation. A *plan* is a method or process.

Here I am going to say that *planning* consist of choosing who, what, how, when, and where of goal attainment. Once a *plan* has been set in motion, *planning* lends flexibility to meet and address unforeseen challenges.

I think I started planning early in life because if I ever said, "Can't," my mother spanked me. So, I had to start planning right away on ways to be self-sufficient and resolve my problems. Thus, it seems that planning has always been an automatic process with me, but I didn't define the parts and sequence of planning until ten years ago.

---

[37] Dwight D. Eisenhower, five-star General in the United States Army, thirty-fourth president of the United States.

A good plan, violently executed now, is better than a
perfect plan next week. – George S. Patton[38]

When my son, Jay, was four years old, he had numerous bouts with sore throats, bronchitis, and tonsillitis. Where I worked, I had no health-insurance plan. My small town doctor told me I should consider having Jay's tonsils removed as that seemed to always be the source of his infections. I looked down Jay's inflamed throat and seeing his swollen tonsils with droplets of pus, I knew right then the operation had to be done. That was the challenge I faced.

I was prideful. Part of that pride meant I was willing to assume my responsibilities, but I had no extra funds for this operation, and no credit. My attitude was simple: my son, my responsibility. So, along with my day job, I sold blood as often as allowed, and I scrubbed toilets at night to acquire the needed funds. Because Jay could come to work with me at night, I incurred no baby-sitting costs. That helped speed up the process. A couple of times, I asked my dad to look after Jay, but Dad was only home on Sunday, Monday, and Tuesday nights. Dad eventually asked me what I was doing. When I told him he then asked if Jay's father was helping. I said, "No." Dad asked me how much I needed. By then I had accumulated all but $75 of the needed funds.

Dad said, "Schedule him. I'll pay the rest of whatever you need."

In preparation, I had already shopped hospitals in the area; the hospitals in Omaha were too expensive. So, right after accepting Dad's support, I scheduled Jay's operation for the coming Friday at a small hospital twelve miles from home. This was a hospital that my mother had helped promote and get built. Everything

---

[38] George S. Patton, U.S. Army General in World War II

went well for Jay. I missed only three hours work at my regular job.

For two months I brooded about that situation. I simply did not like the position in which I found myself. Three months later, I made the decision that I would never again in my life have an occurrence like that. I started on a plan to obtain enough money that I would never have to face those circumstances again. I formed a million-dollar vision.

I didn't have all the parts of "the plan" as I know it now, but I was certain of what was needed and the outcome I wanted. It took about six months, then the plan came together with all the parts. The parts are what I am going to tell you about now.

Planning Paradigm

You've read about some of my ups and downs. My story is essentially the story of anyone's life although my successes and losses might be more extreme than most people will experience. Through it all, I have learned to live, love, earn a fantastic income, lose it all, then start up again. My learning process took time, energy, observation of people, and a study of books. For me, the previous chapter titles, the "Ps,"are the basics leading to a workable planning paradigm. The difficult part for most of us comes in the doing. It's one thing to think lofty thoughts, but quite something else when it comes to activity and working a plan.

Ideally, this planning paradigm would be so natural in one's life that it will execute automatically on the simplest of tasks, like going to the grocery store or getting up and ready for work. The planning paradigm can certainly be used on more complex, lengthy tasks: getting a job, making a career change, moving across country, starting one's own family or business, making a life plan to obtain a seven-figure income, and so on.

I believe that when a person gets this planning paradigm solidly in their life, they will be amazed at how smoothly life goes. Life will become easier, even effortless and joyful! I won't attempt an explanation of how or why this happens, it just happens. I accept it. Often times I've thought, that's the way the universe is supposed to work! When one is in the right place, at the right time, with the right people, working for a worthy purpose, one is in the "zone," as they say in the world of professional athletes and sports.

In our weekend workshops, students study and practice the planning paradigm steps until they become second nature. Here are the steps:

You

The beginning of any plan is YOU: You are the instigator, the energy source, the pilot in command, the captain of the ship, so to speak. I refer you to the earlier chapters on *Presence*, *Purpose*, and *Passion*.

Need or Want

The "captain of the ship" must have a perceived *need* and or *want—a demand*.

With Intention

Noah Webster's 1828 American Dictionary of the English Language clearly defines *intention*:

1. Primarily, a stretching or bending of the mind towards an object; hence, uncommon exertion of the intellectual faculties; closeness of application; fixedness of attention; earnestness. Intention is when the mind, with great earnestness and of choice, fixes its view on any idea, considers it on every side, and will not be called off by the ordinary solicitation of other ideas.

2. Design; purpose; the fixed direction of the mind to a particular object, or a determination to act in a particular manner. *It is my intention to proceed to Paris.*

3. End or aim; the object to be accomplished.

To execute a plan and realize a major goal, a being must have an *intention*, an intention as strong as a metaphorical lightning bolt.

Damn the torpedoes! Full speed ahead!
— David Farragut[39]

What I'm trying to communicate is, you must have the strength to hold your vision and goal in place through criticism, doubt, ridicule, attack, fatigue, or sheer lack of physical strength.

Vision

Create a vision. The vision resolves the perceived need, want, or demand. When I say vision, I mean specifically a spiritual, mental-image picture. I mean a model, typically and most passionately emanating from your heart and soul.

The picture or model in its best form appears 3-dimensional, in full-color. It includes the *feeling* of having attained the object of your demand. For example, if you wish to own your own home, how does it *feel* to have that roof over your head? In the winter? In the summer? When it is raining or snowing outside? How does it *feel* to wake each morning knowing that you own your home, free of mortgage payments?

While the vision might be designed to overcome a problem or challenge in the physical universe, there are no problems, difficulties, or doubts that are part of the vision. The vision is unencumbered, totally positive, unrestricted. *It is made as if the thing or situation desired has already happened.* Once you do that, it has happened!

---

[39] David Farragut the first senior or "flag" officer of the United States Navy during the American Civil War. He was the first rear admiral, vice admiral, and full admiral of the Navy. He is remembered in popular culture for his order at the Battle of Mobile Bay, usually paraphrased: "Damn the torpedoes, full speed ahead!"

Fill in the details of the vision as you wish. There's no right or wrong way to construct *your vision*. Make it with tactile, smell, even with music if that will be more vivid for you. I know some people who just about live in their visions.

The process will still work if you just place the vision close to you where you can see it anytime you want. I put mine to the upper left, about two feet from my head. Access to the vision is *vital*. Some people commit their vision to the written word, referring to it often. This works, too. Writing it down helps bring clarity.

I have heard many successful people say, put a picture of some object you wish to obtain or a place you wish to visit on your mirror, where you know you will see it every day. There's nothing wrong with that and it's helpful for those who are having trouble with creating a spiritual-mental image. The difficulty I find with such physical pictures is that I can't see them all the time. I would have to carry them with me.

The spiritual-mental vision is stronger than anything in the physical universe. It becomes an anchor for your passion; no one but you can take it away. You might be tricked into giving up on your dreams and visions, however, they come right back once you realize how you gave them away or allowed them to be stolen.

One more thing, commit the plan to paper. Write it down. A lengthy or long-term plan might be modified often.

Knowledge and Skill

You may need additional knowledge or skills to accomplish your plan and realize your goal. To fulfill the vision a person must know where and how to acquire expert help. This is where I have to be really honest with myself not letting ego or pride influence my perceptions and actions. I pause to determine if I have the knowledge or skill to accomplish what I want. Guess what? I often seek help.

In the example above with my son, Jay, I was honest with myself when it came to satisfying my demand. I wasn't positioned for fulfillment. I didn't know enough to prevent that or a similar situation from happening again.

Reviewing my options and possibilities, I realized sales people are capable of earning more money than copywriters or producers of radio and TV commercials. Competent sales people are always needed and wanted. They can get a job just about anywhere. So, I enrolled and attended sales classes and sales management courses two nights a week. My good friend, Pat Nolan, looked after Jay for the two hours per night that I was in class. I also read every book I could find on copywriting, advertising agency management, and sales. I practiced and honed my skills during my day job tending my advertising accounts. In Omaha, in the early 1970s, over a four-year period, I wrote, produced, and directed one small account from their initial $8,000 per year expenditure with us to $137,000.

My dad was getting up in age. We had a family rule that the heir had to buy the farm or the estate. He told me I should be looking at buying the farm from him while he could still help me with the financing. At that point I started studying farming, ranching, feedlot operation, law as applicable to the farm, etc. I borrowed money to pay Dad on a handshake from the local banker. Dad cosigned the loan. Banking was different then. There were many such handshake-deals, but there were notes on the substance of the handshake and other paperwork, too.

None of this plan of mine was accomplished overnight. We're talking about three years of study, late nights after my son was asleep. By that time, I had friends in the city who looked after Jay while I attended class.

Dad died a year into the loan contract, but I was only halfway into the execution of my plan. After Dad died, I modified my plan (*flexibility, pliability*). Originally I intended the plan to resolve the challenge of taking care of Jay, so I set a new goal. I decided that earning a million dollars would be my new objective. That would certainly take care of Jay and provide us with much more.

Dad had about $18,000 left of the money that I had paid for the farm, so I was able to use these funds to pay off the bank. With Dad's death, my plan was advanced by about two years.

I also inherited the corn crop from the planting that year. Corn went to market for less than a dollar a bushel. So the best way to profit from my inheritance was to feed the corn to cattle. I hired a professional order buyer whom I knew and trusted to acquire cattle. Then, I went to my banker to borrow money to pay for said cattle.

By this time the loan on the farm was paid off. The banker was not aware that my dad had raised me to be a cattle trader like he was. Also, the banker was unaware that I was experienced in the stockyards of Omaha as a livestock, market reporter. As a market reporter I supplied information and wrote the script for a daily radio and TV broadcast on market prices. I most likely knew more about cattle than most of the men who fed cattle in our area.

The banker informed me that the men in the community were buying their cattle at $28.75 per hundred pounds. His jaw dropped when I told him mine were bought at $23.75, delivered. They didn't calculate shipping costs on that $28.75 so my "delivered" price was even better. I acquired my loan. Of course in a town of two-hundred-fifty people, word spread fast that I was feeding cattle and that I had them laid in my feedlot at that excellent price. The men collected in the local garage-gas station-fuel oil-feed store-hauling company, waiting for my cattle to arrive.

Some of the men just "happened" to drop by my place for a closer look. Five possum-belly trucks rolled in and one-hundred-twenty head of the thinnest, long-tailed, piggy heifers slowly came off the truck.[40] Most of the men just walked away rather than laugh in my face.

The cattle drank copious amounts of water; I gave them some hay and a little grain. The next morning, I turned them into the cornfields. There they cleaned all the corn and stalks from the field. From there they went into the feedlot.

The cattle gained almost four pounds per day for ninety days. The market went up. I laughed my way to the bank making almost $10,000. Jay was six at the time. He cared for five of those calves as if they were his own. After they sold, Jay opened his own savings account at our bank. Neither the banker nor the men in the community were so brash as to laugh at me again. I continued to feed cattle in that manner for the next four years.

When the vision is strong and stable, and you have acquired the necessary knowledge or skills, and or you have surrounded yourself with reliable, knowledgeable people, you are ready to go on with the plan.

Plans are only good intentions unless they
immediately degenerate into hard work. – Peter Drucker[41]

The Mind

---

[40] Heifers with calves that are unlikely to survive birth
[41] Peter Drucker, writer, management consultant, and university professor

The mind has been recording, taking in all thoughts and actions. The mind obeys automatically. The best minds obey their owners; the worst obey anyone or anything. That's why you have to constantly review your visions and goals and not get distracted with negativity. When it is all organized in the mind, the mind then puts all the data into what I call the Setup.

The Setup

So far we've been talking about aspects of the spirit: You, the instigator, the spirit; desires, demands, needs and wants; intention; visions, dreams, hopes, aspirations, feelings, the idea of games, success, winning, joy, and so on.

When the setup, as above, is in place, the power of intention flows throughout the universe of spirit, through bodies, and the physical universe.

The Physical Body

The body, a carbon-oxygen engine burning low-grade fuel at 98.6°, is programmed into action by your setup. Optimally, the body's requirements are clean air, sunlight, nutritious food, water, and rest. Sitting around thinking good, hopeful thoughts will not accomplish the plan. Too much indulgence in dim, dark thoughts can make a body ill. A person must roll up their sleeves and *make something happen in the physical universe*: talk to someone, chop wood, carry water, and so on.

> *It is a bad plan that admits of no modification.*
> *— Publilius Syrus*[42]

---

[42] Publilius Syrus, Latin writer of maxims, flourished in the 1st century

Attainment!

So, you have worked the steps of your plan. With the completion of each step you have come closer to realizing your vision and goal. *Now*, the results you have before you should mirror the vision. However, this is not always the case.

Sometimes I look at the result I have and it looks like a camel when my vision was a horse. So what can I do? Some people stop. They give up, but you won't stop or give up if you have *Passion*.

This is what I do:

The first thing to examine has to do with me—or in your plan it will have to do with you. I take a good look at the conditions, the circumstances being faced, my strengths and weaknesses. Is there enough spiritual, mental or physical horsepower to execute this plan? This requires an honest look and evaluation. Over the years, my personal coaches have helped me greatly in that regard.

The goal, the product of this plan, is it really something that is needed or wanted? Could it be that I am seeking something that is too self-centered, not inclusive of others? Perhaps I am dealing in a passing fancy and I failed to recognize it as such. When I get to the end of the plan, will the expenditure of time, energy, and effort be worth what I have achieved? These are just a few of the possible questions I might need to answer for myself.

Checking the intention, I ask myself, "What am I really trying to accomplish?" Is my intent clear and strong? Did I become distracted along the way? Was my intention one of conviction, honor, and integrity? Was the plan, as outlined, really going to accomplish the greatest good for the greatest number of people in the widest sphere of life?

I check the vision. Was that vision firmly in place or did it dissolve along the way? I ask myself, "Is it clear? Can I see everything I want to attain?"

"Was this a vision of strength, conviction, honor, and the greatest good for the widest sphere?"

If the vision is not for the greatest good for the greatest number, or it's just good for me only, it may not develop.

I check my knowledge, or lack thereof. Is there something that I need to know. I swallow my pride, then take an honest look. If I need to know something or if I don't have the knowledge, I hire an expert.

(When I was talking about my first one-hundred head of cattle in the feedlot, did I have the ability of a professional buyer? No. I hired someone who did have that ability. My neighbors were expert cattle buyers for one day out of the year. When they pulled into the sales barn in Sand Hills of Nebraska with their trucks, do you think the market did not go up $5 to $10 per hundredweight? Yes, it did. So examine what you know and don't know to get this vision with all the parts that are necessary for success.)

Problems arise, as we farmers and ranchers say, from Nature or Neighbors. When they occur they have to be addressed or they will lockup the mind and render it nonfunctional. This is where I have to decide to fish or cut bait, raise or fold, put up or shut up on my dreams and visions.

If there are problems that I can overcome, my knowledge in the area will begin to rise with my experience; the vision will become clearer and more precise. I'll see my way through the plan. If problems don't abate, I know from experience that I am starting down a slippery slope to . . .

Physical Difficulties

Pain, this can manifest as any physical difficulty, headaches, stomachaches, and such. Pain can be emotional, manifesting as anger, frustration, grief, and so on. Pain can manifest as spiritual phenomena, rendering the being itself unconscious like the walking dead.

Upsets

Upsets are the antithesis of setups. Thus, upsets are relatively easy to identify. An upset is characterized by unwanted or inappropriate emotions, just downright unhappiness to a greater or lesser degree.

Most importantly, severe upsets can mean violations of personal integrity, principles, virtues, and standards. Simply stated, upsets are characterized by poor, or dishonest, or inadequate, or total lack of communication, activity, and results.

The good news is that even the most severe upset can be reverse engineered, but it often takes some help from another. A person with a severe upset often won't confront it. Locating the dishonest communication, the secret, and so on, a clever consultant can reverse engineer this upset back to its beginning. When it is all said and done, a person arrives, again, at step one of the planning paradigm, refreshed.

This identification of upset is so important I'm going to mention this example. This is not a political statement. I bring it up to show how an intelligent man with a great need, intention, vision and plan had a problem.

Bill Clinton, the forty-second president of the United States made a decision when he was ten-years old, to be president of the United States—so I've heard. He met President Kennedy at the

White House when he was eighteen or so, and then he renewed this vision.

Clinton attended the right schools, made the right friends, married the right woman, did everything right. He was (and is) charismatic. Eventually, he was elected to the office he sought. Then "power" crept in. He violated standards and codes of honesty and his office. He was impeached. Then came the day we observed him at his lowest point, skirting the issue before him. He attempted to avoid the issue by obfuscating the matter with an idiotic redefinition of "is" on national TV.

It all boiled down to this: "I did not have sexual relations with that woman!"

Really?

Moral: No matter how big you get, seek to live with the truth; don't violate your codes, principles, virtues, or honor in business, with family, or your friends. You may not have the charisma to charm your way out of your predicament.

I know from experience that any failure to maintain the highest principles will make me feel weak as if there is a black cloud hanging above my head. Everything seems to go wrong. My advice to myself is: Seek help whether obtained through professional counseling, coaching, even medical help. I know that if I don't take action I am looking at the beginning phase of a physical illness and, possible, another failure in life.

It's interesting how some of the top executives who are serving jail sentences or those who get fired often times come down with serious illnesses, their dreams and visions collapsed into rubble.

Ken Lay of Enron fame comes to mind.[43] He died before he could be incarcerated.

When the pain is so great that a person can no longer attend to their affairs, they go elsewhere. Not to step on anyone's toes here, but when an ambitious plan fails, when too many dreams fold, people will do such things as quit their job or relationship, hang out with a new crowd, move elsewhere, and so on. There's going elsewhere physically as well as mentally and emotionally.

---

[43] Kenneth Lee "Ken" Lay (April 15, 1942 – July 5, 2006) was an American businessman, best known for his role in the widely-reported corruption scandal that led to the downfall of Enron Corporation. Lay and Enron became synonymous with corporate abuse and accounting fraud when the scandal broke in 2001. Lay was the CEO and chairman of Enron from 1986 until his resignation on January 23, 2002, except for a few months in 2001 when he was chairman and Jeffrey Skilling was CEO.

On July 7, 2004, Lay was indicted by a grand jury on 11 counts of securities fraud and related charges. On January 31, 2006, following four and a half years of preparation by government prosecutors, Lay's and Skilling's trial began in Houston. Lay was found guilty on May 25, 2006, of 10 counts against him; the judge dismissed the 11th. Because each count carried a maximum 5- to 10-year sentence, legal experts said Lay could have faced 20 to 30 years in prison. However, he died while vacationing in Snowmass, Colorado on July 5, 2006, about three and a half months before his scheduled October 23 sentencing. Preliminary autopsy reports state that he died of a heart attack caused by coronary artery disease. As a result of his death, on October 17, 2006 the federal district court judge who presided over the case vacated Lay's conviction. (Wikipedia)

In summary:

- A good plan will take you where you want to go. *YOU* are the beginning of any plan. You are the instigator, the energy source, the pilot in command, the captain of your own ship.
- You must develop a perceived *need, want,* or *demand.*
- You must create a *vision* that represents the outcome of the plan. *The Secret* by Rhonda Byrne is an informative, easy-to-read book that summarizes application of the spiritual-mental aspect of visioning and the law of attraction.
- You must fire up the execution of the plan with *intention* and *passion.* Somewhere along the line you will have to decide the price you are willing to pay to reach your goal. Dr. Wayne Dyer has a good book and an interesting lecture series on intention, *The Power of Intention* and *The Secrets of the Power of Intention: Live Lecture.*
- You must predict the resources you will need, then bring them together. Resources include the acquisition of *knowledge* or *skills.* Acquire or hire, but obtain them you must.
- Operate your physical body—*do something*! The body must be properly fed, rested, and cared for or it will not serve you.
- Finally, the result should mirror the vision or you have some *correction* to tend to.

There you have it. It's been my intention all along that the information herein is both interesting and useful. If you would like to share some success stories with me obtained by reading this book, I'd love to hear from you. If you have questions, concerns, or would like some help with your own plan, let me know. Reach me at <wanda@NeverSayCant.com>.

Epilogue

The first chapter of the book is, *Presence*. The process of living, of accomplishing anything at all, begins with one's presence. I would say, the ability to confront that which is, forms a subset of presence. So, I am wrapping up the book with more examples of confront and presence. It's that important.

Here's a couple of stories to illustrate my point:

Confrontation:

It's my opinion that if a person learns to confront whomever or whatever is in front of him or her, that person can eventually face, and handle, just about anything.

Some years ago, I leased nearly one-thousand acres of pasture from the Federal Government. The property was located in Salina, Kansas. I secured the land at a very reasonable price. By reason of the contract, I was required to fence the property.

By this time, Jerry had become a former husband. He was living in Salina. He needed work, so I hired him as my foreman. Jerry had new fence built, as required. He maintained the fence all around the property, excepting a quarter mile along the neighbor's property. The old fence in question was along the top side of our leased property. Under rural standards, the neighbor's fence would be maintained by him.

I asked our neighbor, we'll call him Joe, if he wanted his fence fixed. Our crew was available; the cost was reasonable; but Joe declined the offer. He felt that his old fence would be adequate in keeping the cattle off his property.

The lease ran five months, from May 30 until October 30, for five consecutive years. Jerry had about one-hundred acres of cane planted in the middle of the property; it was fenced off. If the cattle didn't have enough grass when fall rolled around, they could be turned into the cane field.

About two weeks after the cattle were hauled to pasture, Joe phoned to tell Jerry that he had corralled twenty head of our cattle that had come through the unmaintained portion of fence. When Jerry arrived, Joe wanted twenty dollars per head for feed and care. Jerry gave him a check, then he drove the cattle back through the fence and chased them to the bottom end of the pasture.

When Jerry called for reimbursement, I told him I would give him a check when Jay and I flew over, in the coming weekend, unless I needed to immediately wire funds to his account. I let Jerry know that as far as I was concerned, Joe's demand was nothing less than ransom.

I was busy working between Iowa and Nebraska, looking after the feedlot and cattle there. I told Jerry that he, or maybe he along with one of his friends, should go out every night to check on the cattle. I told Jerry he could just hoot and holler, hit the side of the pickup, and chase them back to the bottom end of the pasture each evening.

Jerry agreed. This would be the best way to address the problem as the fencing crew was gone; it would be costly to bring them back, and I couldn't afford to pay a ransom to neighbor Joe every day.

After a day or two, the cattle were trained to respond to the noise. They just turned around and headed to the bottom end of the pasture. From there, the cattle would graze back to the top end of the pasture, nearer neighbor Joe's property. By the end of the day, the process would be repeated. That routine worked very well. We had no more problems with our cattle getting anywhere close to the neighbor's property.

I would fly down to Salina from Omaha, normally, once a week, in the evenings. I would bring medicine, pay checks, anything else that was needed. I usually flew back to Omaha that night, but sometimes I would stay over, then fly back the following morning. In that case, I'd go to my day job right from the airport.

About a month after that first encounter with neighbor Joe, Jerry decided to work the herd. I drove my pickup to Salina carrying medicine, a branding iron, food, water, and camping gear.

Jay wanted to camp out by one of the ponds. There he expected to catch some large frogs that would become supper. We planned to cook frog legs in an iron skillet over an open fire. If you are an outdoorsman, you might appreciate Jay's idea. However, you must know that I am not a camp-out person. My idea of roughing it is going to an air-conditioned hotel, one that doesn't have a swimming pool or nearby restaurant. Nevertheless, as a mom you often find yourself capitulating if it looks like it would bring joy to your kid.

Five of us, two of Jerry's friends, Jerry, Jay, and I arrived at the pasture entry gate about 7 a.m. We split up. Jay stayed with me.

Jay and I took the pickup to the top end of the pasture where the new fence met the neighbor's old fence. A wire gate had been installed. It was pulled open so it would be easy for the animals to enter the neighbor's property. That was a curious thing because there was no need for a gate there.

I drove to the top of a nearby knoll so I could get a better look. There I couldn't believe my eyes. My neighbor along with two wranglers was driving another twenty head of cattle toward me and the wire gate. The situation had all the markings of some good old-fashioned cattle rustling!

I started honking the horn and hitting the side of the pickup. I didn't know those cows would turn and run as fast as they did. They ran into the guys on their horses. One of the horses reared. The other horse spooked and took off to the side. The change was so fast and unexpected that the riders were nearly thrown. The sight was much like a contrived Hollywood movie moment.

Neighbor Joe was riding lead. He came fast toward the pickup. I sent a series of beeps of my horn hoping that one of the guys would realize something might be wrong, then come to help.

I almost forgot that Jay was in the pickup with me. I heard a fearful, "Mmmooommm" coming from Jay.

I said, "It's okay, Jay. I'll handle this." I stepped out of the pickup.

Neighbor Joe was still riding hard toward the pickup when I stepped out. As Joe's horse slid to a halt, Joe came out of his saddle. A .30-30 rifle came with him, pulled from his saddle holster. Joe hit the ground standing up. He held volumes of anger in his eyes.

I locked in on those eyes. There I stood, face to face, ready to deal with whatever might come my way.

I never took my eyes from his. He was angry, to say the least. Neighbor Joe claimed those were his cattle. He protested my noise making as I could have hurt his sons. Ah, the two rustlers I saw with him were his sons. In my peripheral vision I saw the boys had recovered their horses. They were now heading toward us.

Neighbor Joe cocked his rifle. I stood my ground, still eye to eye.

As we confronted each other, I saw another rider coming hard toward the scene. It was Jerry. He was spurring his horse and slapping it from side to side with the long end of his reins. As he approached us, he didn't bother to slow down. He came off his horse, head first, hitting neighbor Joe in the back. The momentum of Jerry's horse sent it crashing into neighbor Joe's horse. Both horses took off different directions. The two sons who had recovered from the turning cattle, and who were now resting, almost lost control of their horses, again.

Neighbor Joe went face down in the dirt. I hit the dirt, too. The rifle flew out Joe's hand; it fired, but didn't hit anyone or anything. Jerry instantly became the rodeo bull rider he used to be. He jumped up, straddled neighbor Joe, grabbed the collar of his shirt, and began raking his spurs, cussing and calling him names.

I picked myself up, then picked up the .30-30 rifle. Jay, who was in the pickup all this time, started to get out. I yelled, "Stay put!"

Neighbor Joe was screaming in pain as Jerry spurred him from the armpits to the hips, just like he used to do when he was bull riding.

I said, "Jerry! Stop! Stop! Stop! Let him up!" Good grief, Jerry was angry. He could have really hurt the guy. What chaos for a few minutes.

Jerry stepped back to let neighbor Joe up.

By this time, I could see another rider coming on strong from the south, the same direction Jerry had come from. Neighbor Joe was still as angry as could be; we had caught him stealing. He asserted his outrage, those were his cattle, he was going to sue for damages. He was going to call the law!

The rider who was coming up hard now pulled his horse to a stop, then stepped off. Responding to the angry comment about calling the law, Jerry said, "That's no problem. Here's Deputy Sheriff Henry Butler." Jerry bowed and made a sweeping jester with his hat.

Neighbor Joe, caught in the not-so-neighborly act of rustling cattle, foolishly attempted to defend his position.

Finally, the Deputy Sheriff understood the situation. We had trained our cattle to run south at our noisemaking. Furthermore, our cattle all carried our brand. Neighbor Joe eventually calmed. The Deputy ordered him to take the gate out of the pasture by Monday. If there was any reason for Joe to come into the pasture again, he should call the Deputy first. He gave Joe his card.

The confrontation was over. We rounded up the cattle, then went to work as planned. The guys laughed and teased me a lot about tying to get them killed, just because I was willing to stand there facing a man with a loaded gun.

I laughed and said, "I am glad Jerry showed up. However, you should know that I am under divine protection."

Jay followed up with, "Besides that, Mom and I are magic together!"

Presence, Again:

We were having another cold, January evening when I turned down the long lane to the farm. I was surprised to see a familiar car; it was Mary's. Her teenagers had driven the car over and they were waiting for me there in the yard.

I pulled up. The girls rushed to tell me that Jay had burned his face. Mary had rushed him in their pickup truck to the emergency room at Missouri Valley Memorial Hospital, about twelve miles away.

I burned rubber turning around, then headed to Missouri Valley pushing one-hundred miles per hour.

I rushed into the emergency room; there I found Jay on a gurney. Doctor Wilson said Jay wouldn't let anyone help him until I arrived. "Wanda, the hospital is full. We'll treat him and then you can take him home, but he has to be here every day for a change of bandages. Can you do that?"

"Of course," I said.

I could see Jay's face was burned black. His eyebrows and lashes were gone. His hair was burned back about an inch from his hairline above his face. Above and below his right eye, Jay had third degree burns.

Mary was there with me.

I looked Jay in the eyes. I said, "Jay, I want you to look at me, okay? Be here right now, in this moment. No thoughts of the past, no thought of the future, just be here with me in this moment."

I took Jay by the hands. He looked into my eyes. He became very calm.

The doctor applied medication to Jay's face. Jay didn't let out a sound, not even a whimper. We were locked as one, in total presence; the doctor bandaged Jay's entire head. Before the doctor finished, he cut a slit for Jay's mouth, another for his nostrils, and two more slits for his eyes. As the doctor worked, Jay kept his eyes on mine, except briefly when the doctor had to cover his eyes.

When he had finished wrapping Jay's bandages, Doc Wilson commented on how much Jay had calmed compared to how upset he was when he arrived. Then the doctor went on to say, "We're looking at plastic surgery on those openings above and below his eye. And, there may be damage to the eyes that we're not aware of at this time. Nevertheless, I am certain those openings will need surgery."

Jay assessed the doctor's comments; then he repeated the one thing he could always be certain of, "My mom and I are magic; I'll be okay."

We put Jay in the car to take him home. I paid the bill. Mary walked out of the hospital with me. I asked if she knew what had happened.

Jay told her while on the way to the hospital that he was doing his chores, attempting to burn trash in a fifty-gallon drum—one of his regular duties. Right after his chores were complete, Jay and I would be heading out to Minnesota for our weekend ski trip. The wind kept blowing out his match, so Jay put gasoline on the pile in an attempt to speed things along. Just when Jay looked into the barrel to see if it was burning, the gasoline exploded on his face.

Mary went on to say that Jay was making an effort to care for himself by applying ice-cold compresses, but when he looked at his face in the mirror, all he could see was his once familiar face now charred and black. He was bleeding above and below his eye. That's when he called Mary.

On the way home, Jay apologized for messing up the ski trip. I let him know it was no big deal. We could ski another time.

Once we settled in the house, I let Jay know that I wanted him to do Presence exercises with me, at least four times a day for the coming week, perhaps longer.

One of the exercises involved a laying of hands or, in this case, just a finger. The gentle touch helps a person free their attention from a painful area of the body; it allows a resurgence of circulation and life force in an injured area.

We worked on Presence exercises four separate times before the doctor's appointment the following day. After our last exercise, I asked Jay if he wanted a pain pill. He said, "No, Mom. It really doesn't hurt."

The next afternoon, we went to see Doc Wilson; he took us in right away. Jay sat on the table with his back to me; I couldn't see his face when the bandages came off. The doctor stepped back in amazement. He said, "What's going on here? These burns look like they are a week old!"

I asked that he put vitamin E oil on Jay's face. He did. Then the doctor bandaged Jay's face as before. Jay lived for a while on a liquid diet with heavy doses of vitamins A, D, and E. I worked with him on Presence exercises every day.

On Sunday, we met Doc Wilson at the hospital while he was doing his rounds. He redressed Jay's bandages. Again, he expressed his amazement over how fast Jay was healing.

Sunday night was the worst for Jay. He was healing so fast that his face itched like crazy. We continued our Presence exercises on and off until 2 a.m. Jay finally settled down, then went to sleep. The next day at 6 p.m. we met Doctor Wilson at his office.

Doctor Wilson removed Jay's bandages. Jay's eyebrows, eyelashes, and hair were coming back. All the black skin was gone; his face was covered in new, pink skin. The open, bleeding wounds above and under his eye were now scabbed over. Doctor Wilson said, "I don't know what you two have done, but it's very close to a miracle in my book.

The doctor asked, "Has he been in any pain?"

I said, "No. Here are all the pills. Could someone else use them?"

Jay and I continued with our regimen of Presence exercises. Tuesday morning when Jay left for school, his face was covered in healthy skin. His open wounds were well healed, his scabs were gone. His eyebrows and eyelashes were normal. His hairline had returned making it look as if he had attempted to give himself a haircut over the weekend.

I would guess that we spent nearly twenty-four hours, in total, doing Presence exercises. Was Jay's recovery a miracle? Magical? Good science? I'll let you decide. This I know: Presence is a powerful tool; with high level presence, in other words, when one is really being there, a person can succeed in all areas of life.

Resources:

Here I have listed a few of the books, people, and subjects I have turned to in times of need, or in my quest for more knowledge. I had books on the many subjects that interested me: animal husbandry, ranching, farming, medical books on cattle and human beings, aviation, property management, sales, real estate, playing the commodities and stock markets, diamonds and precious metals, and more.

I am not suggesting that others should follow my path; I am suggesting that finding and following one's own path is the better choice. Develop your own reference library; seek the knowledge that will help you achieve your own goals.

The year before Nathan died, he had an appraiser come out to the house and look at my library. The appraiser valued it at $86,000. Since that time, I have boxed all the books, moved a few times, and finally I gave most of them away. When I was in Dallas, I donated many of my books to a Hispanic library. However, I still have a few from earlier days; I continue to buy those books that I need or want, and I never stop learning.

Here are some of the titles I remember; I recall these, particularly, because they contained information that greatly influenced my life:

- *The 7 Great Religions of the World*
- *Auntie Mame* by Patrick Dennis
- *The Unsinkable Molly Brown,* movie script

When I left my first husband I took to reading many books on marriage and raising children. The most important book I found on child rearing was *Born to Win: Transactional Analysis with Gestalt Experiments* by Muriel James and Dorothy Jongeward.

At one time, this was required reading for elementary school teachers.

- *Miracles For Breakfast* by Ruth Minshull
- *Success: Full Living : How to Make Life's Built-In Mechanism of Success Work for You* by Justin Belitz

After I set my goal to make the money I desired, I realized I didn't have much of a clue on how to arrive at it. I started reading everything I could get my hands on. I also interviewed and sought the guidance of people I personally knew who demonstrated financial success. Inquiring as to the what, where, when, and why's of financial acquisition and management I spoke with Ray Motz, "Fat" Middleton, and Richard Day.

Mr. Motz had been a good friend of Dad's. He farmed large plots and operated a feedlot at the home place. Mr. Motz sold Dad's cattle at auction after Dad had passed on. I would go to him for advice in feeding cattle, rotation of crops, and I'd tap his lifelong experience which he was gracious enough to accommodate.

"Fat" Middleton was an older gentleman who ran the local, multifaceted garage, gas station, fuel oil delivery, feed store, cattle hauling, etc., company. He operated several large farms and played the stock market every day. We visited often about those subjects. He was never as brave on other matters as he was on those related to commodities but we had many informative discussions. "Fat" was just a nickname he must have picked up as a child, or maybe it was a bit of a joke as "Fat" weighed no more than one-hundred forty pounds standing five feet seven inches tall. He had a remarkable work ethic arriving usually by 4:30 or 5:00 a.m. and closing shop around 10:00 p.m. "Fat" was, I think, in his seventies when I knew him

Richard Day was my banker. He was kind, patient, and intelligent. Mr. Day owned the bank and if he wasn't busy when I went in to pay or borrow we talked stock market, commodities, corn, gold, and money market. He was the first one to tell me about the country going off the gold standard back in the 1970s. He also talked about the soon-to-be-lifted restrictions that were put in place by the Federal Government, the restrictions that were designed to save people from the devastating financial situation that had occurred in the 1930s. He spoke of the many regulations and changes that seemed to come daily from the Feds.

I was not surprised when he sold the bank to an investment group from the Sand Hills of Nebraska. I lost a good friend and confidant. The new officers really didn't want to do business with a woman. Nathan was around then and though he hardly knew the front end of a cow from the back, the new bankers would only talk to him.

When I became a realtor I studied creative financing and law as applicable to the farm and real estate. I studied sales and marketing with Tom Hopkins, Frank Belcher, and many others. I took advantage of one-hundred to two-hundred hours of continuing education classes each year over the twenty years I sold farms, ranches, homes, acreages, and exchanged properties. Then when the fair winds of the market shifted I entered real estate appraisal work and acted as a general certified appraiser in Iowa, Nebraska, Kansas, and Missouri for several years.

Here's an incomplete list, in no particular order, of some books that I found helpful along my way:

- *How to Win Friends & Influence People* by Dale Carnegie
- *Think and Grow Rich!* by Napoleon Hill
- *The Millionaire Next Door* by Thomas J. Stanley and William D. Danko
- *The Magic of Thinking Big* by David Schwartz

- *Secrets of the Millionaire Mind: Mastering the Inner Game of Wealth* by T. Harv Eker
- *The Science of Getting Rich* by Wallace D. Wattles
- *The One Minute Manager* by Kenneth H. Blanchard and Spencer Johnson
- *The Richest Man Who Ever Lived: King Solomon's Secrets to Success, Wealth, and Happiness* by Steven K. Scott
- *Think Big* by Robert Anthony
- *Who Ate My Cheese?* by John Nichols
- The "Chicken Soup" series of publications by Jack Canfield, Mark Victor Hansen, and others
- Many different books on *body language*
- *How To Choose Your People* by Ruth Minshull
- *How I Raised Myself from Failure to Success in Selling* by Frank Bettger
- *The 7 Habits of Highly Effective People* by Stephen R. Covey
- *Words that Sell* by Richard Bayan

I attended the Dale Carnegie Sales and Sales Management Course as well as courses on communication; also I studied with Toastmasters. Then, having discovered what I needed to know regarding sales, marketing, property management, and so on, I started down a more spiritual path in my studies.

- Sylvan Mind Development, José Silva and Justin Belitz
- *The Science of Mind* by Ernest Holmes
- *Life and Teaching of the Masters of the Far East, Vol. 1* by Baird T. Spalding
- *The Millionaire from Nazareth: His Prosperity Secrets for You!* (and other books) by Catherine Ponder
- The Holy Bible
- *The Book of Mormon: Another Testament of Jesus Christ* by Joseph Smith
- *Tao Te Ching* by Lao-Tse
- *The Bhagavad Gita,* classic Indian Spirituality

- *The Vedas,* the oldest layer of Sanskrit literature and the oldest sacred texts of Hinduism.
- The sayings of Confucius, Chinese thinker and social philosopher
- The Koran, the central religious text of Islam
- *The Lost Years of Jesus: Documentary Evidence of Jesus' 17-Year Journey to the East* by Elizabeth Clare Prophet
- *Rules of Civility & Decent Behavior in Company and Conversation* by George Washington
- *The Celestine Prophecy* by James Redfield
- *Rolling Thunder* by John Varley
- Books by Edgar Cayce
- *A Course in Miracles* by Anonymous and Helen Shucman and William Thetford
- *Lessons in Truth; Christian Healing; Myrtle Fillmore's Healing Letters* by H. Emilie, Charles Fillmore, Myrtle Fillmore
- *Conversations with God: An Uncommon Dialogue (Book 1)* by Neale Donald Walsch
- *Silent Power* by Stuart Wilde
- *Infinite Self* by Stuart Wilde
- *The Little Money Bible* by Stuart Wilde
- *Jonathan Livingston Seagull* by Richard Bach
- *Illusions* by Richard Bach
- *The Prophet* by Kahlil Gibran
- *Heal Your Body* by Louise Hay
- *Quantum-Touch: The Power to Heal* by Richard Gordon and C. Shealy
- *The Power of Now: A Guide to Spiritual Enlightenment* by Eckhart Tolle
- *The Lazy Man's Guide to Enlightenment* by Thaddeus Golas
- *Tuesdays with Morrie* by Mitch Albom
- *Autobiography of a Yogi* by Paramahansa Yogananda
- Dr. Wayne Dyer audio lectures

- *Tibetan Tradition of Mental Development* by Geshe Ngawang Dhargyey
- A study of charisma, a rare trait found in certain human personalities usually including extreme charm and a "magnetic" quality of personality
- Neurolinguistic programming (NLP), an interpersonal communication model and a controversial approach to psychotherapy, co-created by Richard Bandler and linguist John Grinder in the 1970s.

Wanda Novak, still reaching, still growing . . .